Advo

Advocates for Justice

Volume Six of the God Book Series

Copyright © 2014 by Celest and David

This book is not a work of fiction and has been intentionally unedited.

A special acknowledgement for special people.

We wish to thank Maria Nieuwenhuysen in the Netherlands for proofreading for typos and for translating the God Books into Dutch. We would like to send a special "Thank You" to all the other people who have supported our work and helped to bring these books into publication. We also thank Tim for helping us with the formatting of the E-Books and any other technical issues we may come across.

Advocates for Justice

Volume Six of the God Book Series

This book contains information God transmitted to Celestial (Celest) Blue Star of the Pleiades and David of Arcturus.

In this current book God deftly provides new information pertinent to each person's past, their present and their future. He reveals facts about each person's duties here as He speaks about the Advocacy and the individual roles each of us are expected to be personally responsible for. Contained within this book is information no one has been privy to until now. All the previous books have been to prepare you for this specific book.

Catalysts

Foreword

We would like everyone to know some experiences that people have who are reading the God Book Series. Readers are arriving at a greater understanding of life and the transition called "death" and learning of what really happens in the "Hereafters." It is endearing that the Souls of the readers keep urging them to reread the books. If you yourself do not understand why you keep rereading them we can explain this to you because it is important. When first reading any of the God Books many of you are in unknown territory and feeling magnetized to the written word. For some of you there is a sense of familiarity even if it is a vague one about what you are reading. You see, your Soul agreements contained the clause that when a certain gridline intersection had arrived you would be directed, sometimes in a strange fashion, to find out about the God Books and read them. As God just said to us *it was timed to happen this way.*

Some people have said that they knew this somehow, but they never knew how they knew it. Here is that strange Déjà vu effect again. Because your Souls are on their own individual and collective missions they are aware through a form of consciousness called "Universal Consciousness" of what is really taking place. This consciousness supersedes the Super Conscious. The Higher form of consciousness declares that you as "personality" must read and assimilate all that is written as well as all that God writes "between the lines." This has been previously referred to as "God Code."

Those of you who have been rereading the books again and again have found an anomaly that occurs, one that happens to everyone who rereads these books. You have found that the information has somehow transformed itself; it is almost as if you are reading it for the first time. However, you are feeling as if you are receiving more and more information than you did initially. Also, the comprehension needed to understand the writings and to better cope with the emotions that reading these books can cause to rise to the surface, is something so many of you have been trying to understand. The answer is very simple; unbeknownst to you consciously, the more you read them and reread them, the faster you are Super Consciously raising not only your own personal vibration, you are evolving at a dynamic pace, you just don't know it. So the more that you are rereading the more knowledge you are gaining, which means the more your consciousness is expanding. You are looking at everything from a different vantage point; it is from a more elevated form of yourself. This is the Soul "YOU" causing an integration with the personality, effectively bringing you into a more refined form of yourself. Many refer to this as "achieving a state of grace." There are levels and plateaus that you experience when this happens, you may feel as if you are walking on air for awhile and feeling a different type of tranquility. But inevitably the leveling off period begins; it has to be this way. It is important that you come to an understanding about this leveling off period. You still have to live with one foot in each world. It is often at this particular juncture that we see people starting to slide backwards because they are expecting far too much to happen without realizing there are gridline intersections for everything that occurs in life. You need to be content, not complacent, but content with what you are learning *and then* learn patience.

Balance and maintaining your focus are critical. Especially in the times we all now live in. It should be enough for everyone to be content with every step of progress they make. Some people's blueprints, their indelible signatures, require that they take baby steps while others require they take quantum leaps. Regardless of which you feel you take, just know that you are doing the right thing at the right time. The truth of this matter should be self-evident to you. Another thing you can do for yourselves if you feel you simply do not have the time to reread all the books, is to pick up any one of the books you feel is the right one to pick up at the time, and just let the book open to any pages it wants to. There is a soothing balm in whatever words or chapters the book chooses for so many people who do so. In a way, the books act as your divining rod. Although this is the shorter method, we feel rereading the books would give you more of what you need. Think of the God Books as "home." You can go "HOME" anytime you want to!

Even though we know that we were predestined to be the scribes for these books we still do not have any idea what God is going to say. So we, like you, look forward to hearing what is coming on the pages to follow.

Happy **Home**coming ... Celest and David

Introduction (by God)

God ... Hello to all My Earthbound Children; it is endearing for Me and all others of Divinity to see so many hearts gladdened by the realization that YES, My current book of life is now ready for you! Of course you should all understand by now that although it may have seemed to be a long time coming to you, this book is happening as part of the past, present and future spatialness of the NOW. This spatialness is true for all civilizations everywhere except for the people on Earth. But of course these books are being widely read on many worlds. They are teaching tools, you know. The more other civilizations on your own home worlds, as well as other worlds which have not sent any of their races to the Earth Star, learn about what **you** all need to be reminded of, the more they will achieve a continuous state of grace. They will also grow from learning about how much you all have forgotten. In turn those other races will better teach their progeny of the pitfalls occurring on Earth when people become trapped in illusions, in the trap which is also the quagmire of "time." It is quid pro quo.

Yes, it could be a bit confusing to some of you, but once again I request that you leave the linear where it belongs, *it no longer exists.* Instead please try to stay in the Golden NOW of God. When Celest and David first announced to the public that the title for this book is "Advocates for Justice" many shook their heads thinking this would be some type of political rallying or some form of unequivocal writing on the do's and don'ts of dealing with world leaders. Children; I did NOT Create politics so why would I cater to them? I <u>did</u> Create My assistants who were the ones that were and still are part of My delegations of Souls intent on providing truth and justice to and for those who would listen. When this was accomplished on a very grand scale

8

so very, very long ago, the Creator and I desired that these Planetizens would work in tandem with the Starseeds and Walk-Ins destined to spend specific lifetimes on this Earth Star planet. However, as the governor known as "linear time" was erected and effectively blocked My Voice and My Presence from My Children here, the Creator and I convened a tribunal in a different dimension and sought the wisdom of the elders of all other worlds and the Luminescents of each world.

It was there in that long ago period of spatialness that We all decided upon peering deeply into what you term the "future," that far too many Walk-Ins and Starseeds would fall, they would fail themselves and their home worlds. Furthermore We saw that this would be a catastrophic event; one that would cause severe consequences which would ultimately cause the demise of all the human races as a whole. These repercussions would of course impact on the Earth Seeds as well. This was simply not acceptable. We had an instantaneous understanding of all that would be needed to take place here on this planet in order to protect Terra in the future, as well as to protect all other worlds from the contamination that would rain down on Terra.

So many Planetizens implored Us to allow them the opportunities to learn from and by their errors of judgment, rather than for Us to make things smoother for them, that it was agreed that We would not do much to assist them in remembering their destinies. It had been further agreed however that Walk-Ins and Starseeds alike would hasten to answer the calls that their mentors, their Spirit Guides and off-world families would issue to them. Alas, that did not work well at all. Both those groups of Planetizens became so immersed in the murkiness of fantasies disguised as reality, that they lost their own individual autonomy. Although they were once considered to be "human" here because they wore human form, millions of them rapidly disintegrated and became "hu-man." As the reality of the emergence of our Planetizens becoming human became more and more clear to us, the decision had to be to focus on what to do with them. Many no longer had ears that listened; they only had ears that heard. They no longer had eyes which saw the truth; they only had eyes that could no longer see beyond the linear. Their hearts had become cold and callous.

Their minds were entangled in the world of logic and self-gratifying pleasures. They had given over their integrity and personal power in MANY cases, to the dark. So, We arranged to have specific infusions transferred to them through what you term "the Crown Chakra." For some Planetizens the infusions were subtle, for others they were large blasts of a time-released molecule of energy which would send a high frequency pitch and a vibrating type of continuing but periodic oscillation that was relative to a fixed reference point. This point was stored in the matrix of their individual Souls. I suppose you could think of it as "yin meets yang." This was intended to AWAKEN them to their roots, to their individual and shared destinies. In so many of these Children, their very Souls set up some rather sudden mentally or emotionally shocking experiences in order to hasten this awakening process. Many of My Children then began to have near-death experiences, or a turbulent relationship - one that rocked their world, or experienced sudden hardships that they had not been prepared for.

It is amazing, yet sad, that sometimes Walk-Ins and Starseed Children have caused this all to happen to them because they had FORGOTTEN! Needless to say, these "self-help remedies" did not work with everyone. For those Children as well as for the Earth Seed Children, (the Earth Seeds are Earthizens,) We can do no more! All truly good Earthizens are always sent invitations from Me to gather together and evolve; to move beyond the limitations they impose on their lives and their beliefs. *Many are called, few answer.* This book then is designated to assist all Walk-Ins and Starseeds who are here in the present, as well as those of these two groups who will surpass their own expectations of themselves while living a mortal life. It is MY gift to all of you. OK, I do expect you each to be able to see yourselves in this book. I expect you to understand yourselves better, and in doing so you WILL raise the vibration of this planet WHILE having a more expansive understanding of others' foibles. You will also be demonstrating more compassion for others here. You will also raise your own vibrations under the Law of Cause and Effect. Well Planetizens, many of you will encounter new people in your lives in a brief time after you finish this book. You will KNOW if they are Starseeds or Walk-Ins. You will even be recommending this book to the new people you will find in your lives. In your own unique ways you will be "introducing them to God." And your rewards will be grand indeed. *Harvest time always is.*

The melodious signatures that emit from your brainwaves while having the "Ah Hah" moments you receive from "remembering" something you as Soul Super Consciously <u>know</u> in The Hereafters and you realize it is NOW being brought into the present, is quite astounding. I do wish that every one of My Children here on the Earth Star planet would choose to experience this without reservations or hesitations. All knew not to have reservations before entering this Earth realm again. Yet sadly far too many have been caught up in the **washing cycle** of linear time and still do not have the moxie or the desire to find the way to extract themselves from its compelling pull into the abyss of forgetfulness. So today they are finding themselves in "the final spin."

Starseeds and Walk-Ins take notice here... while you still can - many people are progressing more deeply into the NOW. REMEMBER the NOW is part of what exists in the Hereafters, so it will be that when they have left the insanity of this world and the precociousness behind that lays dormant in the hearts and minds of so many people here, they will reenter their Soul's chamber and replay the events of this newly departed lifetime of theirs. *It is the Law.* As the pages of their lives flash before their eyes they will be aware of the footnotes left by them as markers, or reminders for them to remember something they had forgotten, as well as things they originally intended to remember. One of these footnotes will stand out and loudly declare that they missed a big window of opportunity to help themselves in the recently departed lifetime.

That window was to seek, find and then re-familiarize themselves with My words to them. These Souls will not be harsh or cruel to themselves, nor will they be judgmental as so many of My Earthbound Children tend to be. They will simply acknowledge that they let one slip by, an important one no doubt, but just one of undoubtedly many. There are very few who venture into the lesser energy signatures of this world that are adept enough or in tune enough to pick up on all the signs sent their way. These signs were to guide them with the flickering Lights illuminating the path they as Souls had chosen for them this lifetime. So do not be too hard on yourself when you realize you may have been better off to turn right instead of going straight ahead. Each is a choice; none is necessarily wrong, they are all choices. This is what free expression is all about.

I know, I hear some of you saying quietly to yourselves that I must be getting a chuckle out of your misadventures. Just for clarity, I do not receive any satisfaction in seeing any of you struggle, although I will not stand in your way no matter what direction in life you may choose once you have left the realms of knowing. Some of My greatest joys and learning experiences from each of you has been when you have failed to live up to your own expectations of yourselves. Life is about learning and learning can not be achieved without making mistakes. Everyone makes mistakes, more aptly put, "errors in judgment." I just ask that you do not become too proficient at doing so. Those who do will be those who will not be returning to the Earth Star realm any time soon, for they will not be ready to embrace the New Earth's frequencies and altering vibrations. Earth will become An Institute of Higher Learning, much unlike her former schoolhouse planet self you have all come to know. All evolving **Earth** seeds and very importantly all evolving Walk-Ins will be much needed here.

The energetics of the words to follow on each page of this book as you are I hope eagerly flipping each page, will bring you much more of the needed information you require to continue with your missions at this time. I ask you to read each sentence and each paragraph carefully and then move on to the next one. As you do you will see the sequential process of deciphering encoded information that may lay dormant in your **mind's** eye unfold right before your very eyes. My intent here as with all these books of Mine is to take you steadily, progressively into the higher realms of your consciousness where all that you know will come into the forefront of your minds. This is not an easy process and definitely not one that can be done overnight. It would do neither MySelf or YOU any good to short-circuit your steady progress by overloading you all in one instant.

My job is much like that of a farmer. I am always on call, ready to take whatever action is needed to ensure a fruitful crop and this means tending to the crops day in and day out. This is in essence what I do with each and every Soul who has been or ever will be present in My Universe. Right now as many of you are aware there is a weeding process being undertaken; pestilence is being removed. This is happening because there are too many Children who are still not listening to what I have to say. The signs are everywhere for those who choose to acknowledge them, rather than take their normal *duck and cover* routines. Or those Children who chose to hide their heads under the sheets and do as they have always done, wait until the dust has settled to decide which side they are on. You do not understand how much this saddens Me to tell you this, but many of your friends, your family members are not making the grade. They are not following through with what they originally intended to do, what they intended to achieve in this lifetime. So I must pull a few bad weeds starting with any of those who are still associated with the Illuminati ilk. They don't have to be direct descendents; all they need to be is in alignment with them. By "alignment" I mean their priorities do not allow them to care or feel anything about the overall good of all nations, all peoples and of all the diverse lifeforms on this planet of Mine. Sadly there will be many goodhearted people who will be casualties along the way. Each of you knew this going into this lifetime so it will not be a surprise to you when you have *returned home.*

Over the last few decades I, the Creator and the other Luminescents have sent in some of our finest teachers, our bravest warriors and our master healers to change things from **within**, starting from the top all the way down. We have allowed the birthing of a new race of Children to come into this world, the likes of which none have seen here since many days gone past. A great portion of this book will be dedicated to those who proudly wear and have earned the right to be a part of what is known as *The White Rose.* Many will arrive through natural channels; others will arrive in the fashion you now know as Walk-Ins. I will speak more on this later. For now I Salute those of you who have followed through and utilized this great gift of teachings I have shared with all of you through My Celestial-Self and My David-Self. Without their dedication it is likely these books would never have been. My hat is off to them as well as to you. REMEMBER though, I too wear "many hats." Linger through the pages; immerse yourself in *remembrance* of MY Divine Love for all of you.

From My God-Self to your God-Self

Catalyst 1

The Advocacy

God ... OK Children, in My introduction phase of this book I gave you information which I fully expect you to use as the foundation for your understanding of all I will be saying to you. *This is very necessary! You are at critical mass now, so I suggest you build your foundation carefully.* You are standing atop the point of change. All of the Luminescents of all worlds are working in tandem to heal the breech that the falling of the Walk-Ins and Starseeds has created. Some who experienced *the fall* were because of actions that were self-created, yet most were craftily planned by dark people here who KNEW who the Walk-Ins and Starseeds were that were to BE the difference for the Earth Star planet and humanity as a whole. The pure innocence each Soul truly bears is understood and respected without limit by all civilizations on all worlds EXCEPT the Earth Star planet. Problems quickly ensue here as each Walk-In and Starseed arrive whose energy signatures bear the fact that they are not only the heralds of the Golden NOW Child, but are also here to implement the blueprint of the New Earth for the New People. It is simply not only an impossibility but unthinkable that these two diverse groups of Children are capable of hiding their Light under a bushel. They could stand naked in the street in 3 feet of snow while in a blinding blizzard and their Light would still shine with the unearthly Light of God, the Light of the combined forces of all Universes.

Walk-Ins and Starseeds have always been here on this planet. However it was only about 2,500 years ago that the ancient ones who had so long, long before that "time" period began, were asked to form specific Soul Clusters that would be dedicated to emerging on this planet holding

16

on to the eye of the storm while carrying with them an aspect of the Jesus THE Christ Consciousness. These Clusters were composed of all who were signing on as well as those Souls We had selected, each agreed to participate as part of a collective consciousness. Their emergence was to take place when the Earth Star planet had passed critical mass and the Earthizens were just carelessly sitting in the middle of the muddle. This then is when Super Consciously these two groupings all joined together as Tomás sent out the crystal bell tone to have all convene in the Crystal City. The **initial** Agreement between Walk-Ins and Starseeds occurred so long ago that I can only tell you this planet was a very young Child then and the waterways and landmasses were only in their first placements here. They have altered completely many, many times since then. As I stated in the introduction We convened a tribunal and set into motion the plan needed to counterbalance what We foresaw would occur here. The meeting with Tomás and all others of the High Council provided the much needed venue for the Agreement to become part of the matrix of each of those Children's Souls. The Agreement, although known to Us by a different name, here on this planet it is called *"The Advocacy."* This is where promises made and promises kept could be said to have been "written in stone."

EACH of YOU HERE TODAY *was there then!* This is a secret that has long been withheld from all of you, at least those of you who are incarnate today. It is only NOW per the Advocacy agenda, that you are permitted to be consciously aware of this. Prior to this gridline intersection so few of you whether Walk-In or Starseed, were able to cope with this awesome knowledge and resulting responsibility. The planet has been in emotional turbulence, in physical distortion and Spiritually challenged and YOU were not prepared to hear this truth. During the active espousal declaration which was not limited by anything linear of course, WE drew up YOUR

17

Declaration of True Independence. We do not write per se, but using pure energy and of course telepathic communications with geometric signatures as Our guidelines, you EACH helped to write the founding statement as the founders of liberty for the Earth Star planet. We at no time attempted to influence one another; that is simply not done here. We know perfectly well it happens on Earth YES, but this did not take place on Earth! Thank heavens for that. One of My Sons, Jesus THE Christ, oversaw the commitment signatures which you all gave to Us. In the most basic sense the plan was simplicity itself...

"Do not divide and conquer. Bring together all those you can and form an indomitable force of unity. Love well, be loved well and bring the Souls together to form an unbreakable circle of truth and justice and do so in the name of God." *Love* is the anthem, the SONG of allegiance declaring loyalty and personal and planetary evolution for all. However, it is also the antithesis of all dark beings regardless of what part of their hierarchy they are. Under the auspices of ALL Universal Laws, all Beings in all worlds are permitted to know what We are doing. In this particular instance it meant that of course the "dark planet" Beings knew of the Agreement. The reason this is permitted is quite simple.

The Creator foresaw that in all fairness to each Soul who is trying different experiences to grow from, it was of primary importance that each Soul be permitted to deal with not only Lighted Beings, but to learn to deal with the dark. Dealing with the dark is an unsavory task, I know that very well. However if all you know how to do is walk in the Light and never encounter any devious obstacles or less than worthy people, what will you learn? You will learn very little for you will not amass necessary experience! Therefore Universal Laws reflect that concept; for they are the purveyors of Eternal Truth and GROWTH through EXPERIENCE. OK now, if you are not yet fully understanding what I am telling you, or if the impact of what I AM telling you is a bit overwhelming, then please read and reread this Catalyst as many times as you need to. Of course there was always the rather slim possibility that even the dark Beings and their contaminated hu-man counterparts might have been swayed by the sheer force of the overwhelming Love and Light that each of you then and now possess.

However those with badly damaged psyches would not see or feel the Love and Light. They would only be in fear for something greater than themselves was present. That always unfortunately has caused an inner rage in those people; one that ultimately resulted in the maiming and death of many innocent people. *Many have died so that others may live ... again and again and again.* Exposing the dark to the Light is always a tumultuous experience, for both sides. **You can not be aligned with what you are not**. Nor can they. OK, so you each toddled off on your merry way while bearing the seal, the Code of God - the Honor of the Creator and the beauty and love of Jesus and His beloved spouse Mary Magdalene. Lifetime after lifetime you followed the Agreement and tested yourselves mightily in order to determine your own strengths and weaknesses. Your mentors ALWAYS are in attendance, prepared to assist and console and do whatever is necessary in order for all of you to adhere to the Agreement and **never give up.**

You each wrote certain codicils in the Agreement; these were chosen by you and overseen by your mentors. We have for Our combined parts worked diligently to assist you each in securing your success. Some of your victories may seem small to you, but We do not see anything you do as "small." Each victory is part of your life-force, part of the integrated YOU. Each perceived failure is really no failure at all. That is **YOU** being too hard on yourself, as usual.

They are simply experiences that you eventually rework until such time as you succeed in your quest. This too is part of the Advocacy Agreement. The Agreement does not ask you to be perfectionists; it simple asks you to be realists and **accept what you can not change.** The Agreement you each signed can not be nullified; the only true exception is if you ever truly believe that "I've had it ... just get me out of here!" At that point your wish is granted. However to date, no one has done that. Although from time to time I do hear a loud grumbling, don't I Celest? NO, she is not the only mutterer in the Walk-In groupings. However she, just as most of the others in that grouping do, do become tired and at times overwhelmed by the lack of support and the resistance to change they encounter in other Walk-Ins AND among the Starseed groupings.

Sometimes though, even though she as a very evolved Soul, she must act-out and do some serious releasing of pent-up frustration. One time I could have sworn I heard one of My Wolf Children challenging the Beast and ready for immortal combat again. But Tomás assured Me it was not a wolf, it was just Celest. I can not say if that caused Me to feel better or not! Her Agreement just as yours, calls for you all to have unlimited patience while you are incarnate. OK, the hostile forces have their own agreement, you know. Theirs however is bound by death, dismemberment and eternal mindless torture if they fail to adhere to the ad hoc agreement designed by the darkest and earliest of the Illuminati. They are to devour the Spirit of all those they can here; IN PARTICULAR Walk-Ins and Starseeds. Earth Seeds have always been easy pickings for them, unfortunately. Those demon riders, who We also call "Shadow Riders" attempt with all the force they can muster to break the Spirits of all those they can. If all else fails then their instructions are clear; take their life. It is known by them as *death by destruction.*

However, it is well known by the dark inhuman agents that the vast majority of Starseeds and Walk-Ins do not consciously remember these ancient foes, at least not while in the incarnate state. Yet again I refer you to the Advocacy Agreement. In this hallowed document it is fully explained that NO, you shall not consciously remember those who have caused you grievous harm in past lifetimes. It does state though that **_SOME_** of you shall through clairsentience FEEL the ancient nemesis' visibility when encountering them in this life experience. A select number of both your groupings did indeed request that a type of self-monitoring system be installed near the core of the matrix of their Souls. This system was to function as a "direction finder;" one that would allow certain faint or at times vague memories to stir within the minds of these seekers. Essentially this means that when exposed to certain people, places or things that go bump in the night, these seekers would immediately be aware that one who was a "rogue bear" was once again loose and intent on causing GREAT harm. I use the term "rogue bear" intentionally; it is a person, usually human but controlled by the dark, who is vicious, lacks self-control and lives apart from the world where the Spiritual Children live. It intimidates, has no basic Spiritual nature and feeds in a sense by gorging itself off the helpless victims' energy, while devastating those persons' minds. So it is that these seekers sought to retain their ability to know WHAT was coming in order to serve and defend not only themselves, but others in their Soul Clusters. It is interesting when a seeker and a bear encounter one another. We have observed this millions of times, and when the seeker is one who carries the direction finder, then it is that both of these Beings KNOW who the other is. It is basic knowledge which does NOT include gory details which could sully the minds of the seekers.

The Advocacy Agreement is very clear about how much you should know and **WHEN**. You each agreed that when this gridline intersection you are now living in came into materialized time, this was when you would once again be privy to this document and WHY. You have each been experiencing edgy sensations; angst at times and almost looking over your shoulders expecting "something" yet you could not put words to what it was. What has been happening is that you have become Super Consciously aware that you are in countdown mode; you are racing against the universal clock. One of the greatest pitfalls that both your groupings have had to learn to contend with is to always use wisdom, NOT logic, when determining which action to take.

Logic is but a stalling point; it holds you on the precipice of formulating right actions. There you may be stalled for most of your life. Wisdom however is the accruement of knowledge and transmuting it into phases of your own personal evolvement, thereby effectively assisting in the needed transformation of the planet. Wisdom is visible as your conscious and Super Conscious's accumulated knowledge of life. It is all that you have learned because of a selected sphere of activity which has been gained through experience. The Agreement is filled with reminders of using wisdom not logic. Or I could simplify this by repeating a phrase that My Celest-Self uses; she tells people, "Knowledge is wisdom in a training bra." I leave you to mull that one over!

Oh Children, I have watched both groupings struggling for so many years now, regardless of their chronological ages, waiting for that SOMETHING greater than themselves to shine the Light into this ever-changing world. Well, in great measure thanks to the Advocacy Agreement which you each signed, YOU are the "SOMETHING greater" that is shining the Light of all Lights into this world. STOP demeaning yourselves by feeling that you are not doing enough! Please make a note, write a letter to yourself and each day take a nano-minute and write down just one wonderful heartfelt thought you have each day. *This is where the "difference" lies.* Yes Children, this technique too is part of the Advocacy Agreement.

One aspect of your missions in the here and now is to be the fulcrum, the catalyst, the Light of clarity that brings *remembrance* of all I am telling you today and share it with others who are receptive to OUR truth. "Ours" is the collective. It is yours and Mine and also belongs to all the others who gathered together in the great hall. It was here in this chamber that you all chose to be a formed total of United Beings; to be a Beacon of Light in the vast darkness when all sanity had appeared to have left this Earthly realm. Look at Me, I have worked with you each for so long that I can not remember when I had a more ubiquitous collective audience as I now have with all of you who are reading My words. I want you each to understand that the Advocates for Justice are *you.* The Advocacy was Created when the collective of all the Soul Clusters gathered together under the umbrella of the OverSoul, which is the greater "I AM." You should remember this term from previous books. If you do not please refresh your memories for I have much more I wish to share. OK, now part of this agreement was the clearly defined explanation about how much each of you would be permitted to remember at any one given time. Each of you has stored all your accrued knowledge within your Soul's matrix. This can be accessed by you independently; but it will only be permitted for you to do so when you have reached an apex, a turning point in your lives. I have told you before that nothing is ever lost or destroyed. All matter, all forms of energy and yes thoughts are energy, are reused, refined or re-assimilated into the Universal pools. You could call it recycling at the highest level. "Waste not, want not," is a truism of itself.

The desire for so many who have awoken is to satisfy their curiosities about their previous incarnations and understandably so. Per the Agreement, some of what you ask about will be answered, but not all. However, if at any time any of Divinity such as your guides and mentors, your Master Teachers or even Myself decides for one reason or another that you are not ready to receive the sought after information, then you will only be given an aspect of the Greater Knowledge. Both Walk-Ins and Starseeds are curious Children at times. Your quest for knowledge is astounding. Your methods of finding it are a little haphazard and MUCH too logical at times. You can scan the internet, attend all the Spiritual social functions you want, interact with others of like-mind, but your best source of truth is through solidifying your connection with your own Soul Voice. Soul will never lie to you and already knows before you do what it is you are searching for.

The Advocacy is here to support you in all your efforts and is the very foundation your life-force has assisted in Creating collectively. The Agreement brings the feeling of "home" as well, so never feel as if you are alone in your efforts. You are now in the gridline intersection of the "timeline" when all things material will be seen for what they are and all things that are Spiritual will overcome the material world. The Spiritual inner-Self is self-fulfilling, replenishing and not of this Earth. The material world is the paper doll; it is the cutout many of you have become too accustomed to feeling was the essence of all that you are. The physical vehicle you inhabit is but a small portion of all that you are. It has limitations. As Light Beings, as Immortal Souls experiencing a physical lifetime, you feel confined and restricted. That dear Children is why you are *earning* your *new* Light bodies. This was agreed to well in advance of your placing your indelible print onto the Advocacy Agreement. Promises made and promises kept. You must do the work necessary to find it within yourself to exist in a continuously fluctuating and expanding state of grace. And to do so requires your willingness to fulfill your personal as well as planetary destinies. Each of Us has a part to play; you agreed to this in your last Soul Contract before you incarnated again. There, that was My pep talk for those of you who are following through with your missions of reacquainting yourself with your SELF. As for the Walk-Ins and Starseeds who are still trapped in the lures of illusions and are faltering badly, they can not participate as true Advocates in the time of NOW. Therefore, unless serious changes are made by them FOR them before the very end of this year, their names shall be removed from the Agreement. In other words, they will be on their own.

So long, long ago, far before your earliest remembrances, We worked together to bring forth ideas and aspirations of where the human race and this world were to be throughout their growth state. Plans were made and We thought about all possibilities and what the eventual outcome was to be. Many plans had to be reworked though. This was because of numerous failed attempts at inspiring Walk-Ins and Starseeds occurred. This was due to the lack of determination of the people themselves to seek the Spiritual way of living. Of course it did not help that true Spirituality flew out the window every time these people were immersed in the lower density thought-forms. Unfortunately too many of the Children of this world fondly adhere to these even now. In the past it was not all their fault. Today it is; personal responsibility is everyone's moral principle ... or should be. Massive changes are underway that were implemented far, far away and long, long ago in the timelessness of the continuum. You are yet again the heralds to move these events forward. OK now, since so many are faltering We have out of necessity had to modify the original blueprint design and choose a much harsher course of action. I am counting on each and every Starseed, every Walk-In, to become more than you have ever been before. You not only signed the Advocacy Agreement, you **are** the Agreement!

In the Earth Star realm I need you to achieve a higher level of understanding and maintain it for extended periods of time. The more you do the more natural of a life in this new form of alignment with your Higher Self will become. And the brighter your personal Lights will shine. Go about your business every day with one focus on your minds, to BE the Light and to BE Spiritual Beings in physicality. Remember please, the correct stance here is to walk with one foot in each world. You have prepared for this. We have tutored you and shown you every possible scenario and its eventual outcome. All of humanity has chosen their futures whether by thought and action, or the lack thereof. At this point it no longer matters. What does matter is that you call in during your waking moments as well as your nighttime visions, more of what you already know but may not be consciously aware of. Just issue the call for the information and if it is in alignment with the Agreement you SHALL receive the answers. In one form or another.

Teams of specialists are standing by awaiting your call. They will be patient only a little while longer. Choices must be made and the time is now. Commit yourselves to your cause or We ask you to move out of the way. In so doing others may come forth and assist the rest of you in ushering in the New World for the New People who are waiting to come in and be change preceptors. The Advocacy is a compendium of likeminded Souls; it means that each of you reading this is an integral part of this. But if for whatever reason if any of you find it more important to hold on to fears and doubts, Earthly possessions, or dwell upon your mortality instead of your Spiritual growth and its newfound wisdom, then you are no longer needed here. We have no more time to lose. Tomás and Others of the High Council are willing to hear your grievances if you feel you have been unjustly thrust into something you feel should not have occurred. But if you chose to approach them, **make sure** you do so for all the right reasons. Right action equals justification not the other way around. Be sure to have quantified your thoughts. *They do read minds you know!*

What I would like to do is to take a moment and tell you about yourself, your Self that IS all it can be in every given moment. There were many Souls who were passed over for this lifetime for many reasons which I am not prepared to divulge right now. You, however were chosen. Whether it was because of your fortitude, your knowledge, or your ability to reach others who will need your strengths now, there were valid reasons. Not everyone can be a Walk-In, not all are be able to cope with the massive changes that occur upon the moment of entering this dimension. Whatever your course you chose for entering this realm you did so of your own free expression. We will ask you to do certain things, but we will never force you to do anything against your will. This was explained in great detail when you all put your hands up and volunteered for this mission. In other words if you haven't guessed it yet, *you all had what it takes to be here now.* As I stated earlier, you ARE the Advocacy. That alone should give you comfort and strength.

As Advocate General I can see what lies ahead for each of you and what I see is green pastures and crystal clear waters. But this will not be for some time to come. First we must get there from here. I can not do it for you; it was never My responsibility to do so. This is why you are representing Me on this world. If you can not hold it together many of the human races may soon become extinct. Although I said, "MAY," I do not see this occurring for you shall NOT fail! I wish you could all see yourselves when your minds are not cluttered with useless data and trivial thought patterns. Your Lights are like prisms of rainbows swirling and twirling and intertwining with All That Is. Your life-force is sustained by these moments. It is as if you have finally found your way home from a place far, far away. You become tranquil, serene and in that

27

moment you know that everything is going to be ok. I can show you the way, I can leave a candle burning in the window, but you must be the one who reaches out and issues the calls.

The Advocacy, "a fortuitous joining of minds and Souls for the distinct purpose of combing forces to make a difference at a time when it is needed the most." The Advocacy program was also designed to expand you both Super Consciously and then **Magna-Consciously** when the need had arisen. You are all intended to be a part of something greater than yourselves, in fact greater than all of Us. We will work together to bridge the division. The division resides between that which is the Spiritual realm, where all is known and understood and that you all are now very familiar with, and the physical realm where you **perceive** there to be limitations on what you can or should be able to achieve. Far from the truth is that you are in any way limited or confined simply because you have a body which can be frail at times and erroneously perceived as Earthbound only.

Far too many still see the world around them in black and white. Please lose this perception. Interwoven in the sands of time is every minute monad of energy that has ever been privileged to be placed upon the place you now call "home." Feel it, sense it, and look beyond the veil, for in truth there is no veil left to hold you in bondage. Rise up to the challenge of Creating a better world by being a better you. There are tendrils of mystical magic weaving through every energy streamer and all that is needed is for you to open your eye, your third eye that is and then you will see. And then you will begin to remember all that you need to at the present time. You are the catalyst for change. You are the warriors; you are the healers and you are the teachers who can help others to touch their Spiritual side. <u>You do this by thought</u>. Intent is everything so let yours be glorious, let the thoughts also be My presence within you.

As we meander through the essential truths being sent to you through My words, try to calm your intellects and feel the essence of My words. Open your hearts and see yourself expanding taller, leaner and faster. See the myriad colors of Light emitting through you. Become one with them; send them out into the world around you. Place them carefully and gently upon all that your senses absorb. Imagine the world pristine and beautiful, her beauty beyond anything you have ever seen before. Feel the connection amongst yourselves and embrace Our inseparable oneness. Stop looking through rose-colored glasses, awaken a new you, a higher essence of you. This is what I ask of you each and every moment of the rest of your stay here. If you can hold onto this state of knowing then you will be able to see the changes unfolding all around you. You will be open to new ideas; new thoughts will enter your minds replacing the old outdated ones. You will feel the energy of the force within. That force is the indomitable Spirit which drives you forward and Creates anew.

We started this journey together, you and trillions of other Souls. We are at the finishing line for this chapter in your book of life. Do not give up on your SELF now. We are watching so many people flailing about, unmotivated with no direction or purpose. Never perceive yourself as small or insignificant and unable to enact change. You can achieve anything you set your sights upon. No, I am not talking about fame and fortune and all those other Earthly distractions. What I am referring to is Omnipresent Immortal Souls which each of you IS. Let Soul visibly enter into your domain, I know many of you have already reached this Divine understanding with your Soul Voice. Remember to check your Sources so you will never be fooled again by those who hide in the shadows, they and the rest of their minions. Trust your instincts; they will guide you far better than any other person who feels they know you. My Children, let there be Light, let you be the Lights illuminating THIS WORLD.

When this plan was conceived so very, very long ago it was decided that out of necessity We would have to place a great many of you in positions of power. Those of you who are doctors, nurses, engineers, biologists, mathematicians and so forth are intentionally where you are now. Especially those Walk-Ins and Starseeds who are working so diligently to awaken others. Each of you no matter what your trade or profession is or was, have the distinct advantage of being able to reach others whom you may not have always had contact with. The others are as many of you were, searching for answers, trying to find purpose and meaning to their lives. They are waiting for the chimes to sound to awaken them to their purpose and ultimately guide them to their destiny. Share a soft word, a smile. Lead them to the oasis by the sparkle, the shine in your eyes. None of you can do it all on your own. I need you to pick up the slack for those who have fallen into the cracks of mortality.

I dedicate this catalyst to all true *Advocates for Justice* everywhere ... *God*

Catalyst 2

The Leagues of Extraterrestrial People

God ... OK now, the more you learn about yourself the better prepared you will be to not merely understand others' situations, but you will see how and why all preparation has been vitally important to all of you who are **ME.** You will see how continuing to be yourself and finally appreciating all that you do for just cause, is in accordance with Universal Laws and with MY own wishes for you to further integrate yourself as SOUL, with ME. In this manner in just a brief time you will be on the threshold of experiencing ME in YOU. No, I do not consider this to be a particularly profound statement. However as always human languages lack the core meanings which We use off-world. In the days past, in this life experience, you have from point to point in your life felt unbelievable jubilation, the Lightness of Being and at times tears of joy for no apparent reason. At least not apparent to you, that is. Although there are some among you who immediately realize that this is when you as Soul are connecting ever further with Me as Soul, most of you do not or have not yet understood this. The most simplistic approach I and others who are part of the collective of Divinity have in integrating with each of you is to simply slowly but continuously send fragments of Ourselves to you.

Here is a basic example: in your home during the day for instance, you may not see all the motes of dust that naturally swirl through the rooms. But if you would shine a very large flashlight in different areas you would soon see that these motes are everywhere. Just because you may not be able to see them without some type of device to assist you, does not mean they are not there. No, I do not consider Myself to be a mote of dust, although dust does serve its own purpose. But We simply send specific fragments of

Ourselves to you each which then not only integrate with your own Soul Essence, but also strengthens Our familial bond. I expressly used the term "specific" fragments; each fragment **is** part of the collective of Divinity. As such each carries infinite memories which trace back to the very core of Our individual existences. So We imbue you with these, BUT We only use the "match-point process." This process is a unique leveling of energies predicated upon the individual Soul maturity, what the individual's present state of personal evolution is at any given moment and individual DESTINY. These sections or portions of Ourselves can be perceived as motes of dust because each seems to be minute individually, yet when they collect they cover great spans of areas. As a collective they can be SEEN. Do _you_ SEE?

It is in this manner that none of you receive too much of Our energy signatures, you can not be overloaded. Throughout this continuous process though, Our energetic signatures which are part of Our energy beams, pass into the physical vehicle. They then extend themselves throughout the body then gather in smaller particles within the matrix of your Souls. This assists in amassing regenerative procedures which are a major priority; now more so than ever before. All of you in each of the two groupings, remember although I said two groupings each grouping is comprised of hundreds and thousands of diverse Souls, is slowly acclimating to the new Earth Star energies here. It is vitally important that you each understand the NEED, the absolute NECESSITY of body, mind and Spirit aligning with these new energies. This is one reason so many of you seem to tire much more easily than you have in the past. OK, the former energies which have been laden with toxicity and with a large layer of illusions and unmitigated fear atop them forming a blanket of ill-health and insecurity, is what you have been born into and walked into. Our wondrous team of off-world doctors and nursing personnel tend to each of you day and night.

Yes, of course they are multidimensional Beings, yet they know you each and have done so, *for as long as you have been.* Their missions have been awesomely complicated; for they must adhere to the Laws while still providing proper medical attention. For the last six years in particular, they have been carefully assisting Our fragments in replacing the darkness of the former infusions you have all been subjected to, with the necessary new qualities and elements which are infinite, rather than finite.

As these new energies continue to form concentric IMAGES of themselves throughout all the organs of the physical body, the intellect must prepare itself for the incoming energy exchanges. The intellect has no problem with this "switchover" as long as it is soothed into the understanding that this is a necessary element to ensure the survival of the body and the enhancement of the mind center. As a result of this smooth and continuous infusion the intellect is assured that it too will survive. Although there is no downside to this procedure, it is as the physical vehicle is adapting to the enlargement of the Light cells that the former smaller and rather congested cellular structure undergoes a different type of metamorphosis. Most of you find that you are viewing things differently while this ongoing process arrives as a culmination of its own higher vibrational level. Essentially the former cellular structure is undergoing a breakup of lesser, denser energy molecules. Those former cells then split into isolated and at times conflicting elements and CAUSE the mind to see things more differently. You see they can no longer feel a sense of cohesion with one another because they have been deftly replaced with a higher level of Light energies. The ones that are now displaced then dissipate by being passed through the body during the bodies' own natural elimination process.

This then is where the medical teams' work is critical. When you are on your own home worlds none of this type of imbuing Our fragments is necessary. At home you are One with Us, yet you are **many**. Yet again all that is occurring with these energetic signatures of Ours is in fact written into the Agreement. It would simply have been impossible for all of you to survive in this present TIME you are living in without the necessary implementation of these energies taking place. No, unfortunately We are not able to do this type of procedure with Earth Seeds. I should correct Myself here; this procedure is not applicable for <u>almost</u> all of them. Over the last 150 years it has been heartwarming to Us to actually feel an Earth Seed reaching out to make some type of contact with Us. This usually happens to them when the world of logic and religious idiosyncrasies has failed them. In desperation they seek answers, solutions or help and basically feel that maybe, just **maybe,** there really is a world beyond logic. A few of them do go on to make slow progress in understanding the world beyond this world. Although I would love to see them all do so, I am realistic about this. I take what I can get! Many of you Children have developed long term illnesses as a result of the noxious gasses being sent into the atmosphere as well as the gasses arising from deep, deep Earth due to the parasitic process called "fracking." In the cases of individual destines being at stake, the medical teams work tirelessly to ensure that you will be able to complete your missions here on the Earth Star planet. Obviously this is a different situation for those who agreed to experience various illnesses as part of their Soul contracts. However, even for these Children the off-world health teams work in tandem for their benefit. They continue to do so in order to allow these Children the opportunities to continue to evolve THROUGH and BECAUSE of the health experiences. And yet these afflicted Children go on to teach others with similar experiences as well. No, these "frequent flyer" trips of yours to this planet have not been easy. Tending to the physical vehicle is one thing, but tending to millions of minds is another!

Even when one's body is in a healthy or even semi-healthy state it is the mind which is the springboard for the Soul that must be carefully nurtured. Here Children is where all but a few Planetizens foolishly place themselves in jeopardy. OK now, because you are each either Starseeds or Walk-Ins you find yourselves in rather unique circumstances here. Here you are on a planet you temporarily call "home," yet very little actually reminds you of your own true homes. The term "extraterrestrial" in its most basic form simply means, "more than Earth." It is nothing else if not self-explanatory, or it should be! Yes, you are **each** extraterrestrials. If you have not realized that then you must have missed My billboard! "Planetizens" are citizens from other worlds, other Universes. "Earth Seeds" are citizens OF and from Earth. You are each part of the culmination of extraordinary extraterrestrial people. Understand please though, Earth Seeds are extraterrestrials too. This is so because they are citizens of a different world, do you see? If by chance someone approaches you and remarks "you look alien," then I suggest you reply, "Thank you."

Also there has been enough foolishness taking place among Planetizens, do not add to this by suddenly trying to figure out what your home planet is! Those of you who should know or should remember will. Please leave it at that. The minds of all Starseeds have been struggling for each lifetime, especially this one, to overcome the suffocating blanket of ideology and logic run amuck. I ask you one and all to please remain detached from logic; it is not the upscale neighborhood many of you THINK it is. For the last 20 years, more and more of you have been able to rip asunder that callous veil of intentional hyperbole and "come into your own." It has not been an easy process for you, I know that. Remember, I am here with you as well. I ask that you do not try to take quantum leaps in your learning and re-remembering process. Rather, be content to "just **KNOW**" that you are progressing in spite of your

FEARS that you are not. Yes, I most certainly do see how many people you have had to sever ties with here, and I also see how many more you still will. Be advised that many of these are Starseeds as well and just accept the fact that they have **fallen** and are not getting up. Learn from the errors in judgment they have made in this lifetime. It will assist in teaching you what NOT to do. Do <u>not</u> judge them! Taking an assessment of themselves is their own individual job to do. It is not your business! You arrived on this planet in whichever manner was deemed most appropriate for you in order for you each **TO BE** here on the scene *NOW*. You are now in the midst of a resurrection that is afoot. It is your own resurrection! You are indeed each a golden Phoenix rising from its own ashes. Your missions both individually and collectively, are to continue to assess the situation here and make it better. **YOU** are My proof that this world is being made better. Your thoughts are helping to Create the actions that are ongoing here. Without your thoughts life here would have become a void. You are all ordinary people contending with extraordinary pressure. OK, remember please, the greater your truths and the greater your thoughts the greater the damage is that you are inflicting on the dark energies.

The new Earth is already in her infancy state; you are to be part of this period of growth. You will do so *Now and beyond the constraints you have experienced here on the Earth Star planet*. Although even the smallest thought can turn the tide of world events, it is when those small thoughts radiate from Earth collectively that miracles are Created. Use your thoughts from now on in <u>*unlimited*</u> fashion. Children, you are the wind, the sea and the sky. Multiply your thoughts on a cosmic sized canvas; think BIG! You can do no wrong in this matter. It is what you accomplish here through simple mind-thought and sheer determination to assist, which will be your own individual and collective <u>**legacy.**</u>

For the rest of your mortality I ask that you remember that in harmony We shall walk again, I said that and it is true. You must all strive to find harmony in your lives by whatever positive means you feel is necessary. For some of you it will be as simple as "Being." In a crowded elevator or a racing subway train those of you who are the most balanced can find peace and harmony while remaining detached from all that goes on around you. No, I did not say "aloof," just detached. Other people will be directed to find quieter places to live and other means to support themselves. One part of your most critical mission of all time here is to be the record keepers for all that you see, feel, and hear. Remember please, that task alone sends vital information back to the rest of your "home" team and further alerts them to any further disturbances within the Force. "Force" means ... organized chaos, which is CREATION. "Force" is also the continuum. By now you should all know the difference between organized chaos and disorganized chaos. I ask that you contemplate upon this for a time for it is important to your own personal growth. Now do you understand why it is so important to *bear witness*?

Now, I want you to consider why so many of your fellow Planetizens are falling. As individuals begin to awaken many will start seeking answers to *the meaning of life*. This is simple; yet even the most brilliant of minds can not always see what is right in front of them. It is not complicated Children, it means that LIFE HAS MEANING. Instead of acknowledging this fact to themselves and moving forward to actually <u>having</u> a life, many of the Earth Walkers start reading, listening and absorbing everything they can find in order to locate this long sought answer. Unfortunately they are not staying in the flow and allowing their own Soul self to direct them. Furthermore they encounter pseudo teachers who lead the seekers astray. Far too many of these seekers become mesmerized by these teachers, not knowing that these men and women plagiarize others' teachings and exhibit exhibitionistic traits. I ask each of you to tell Me what it would require to have your other brothers and sisters start **Checking their Sources?** The shadow riders are nothing if not devious in their ability to be the masters of illusion. They sow just enough truth in what they tell people to misdirect the unquestioning eye from reading between the lines. Once fooled it requires sheer determination on the part of the individual to break through the illusions.

As a lifetime member of the Leagues of Extraterrestrial People it is your duty and your responsibility to question anything that gives you reason to reconsider your beliefs. After all, this is Earth in the present changeover period, not yet the completed future tense of herself. Pause when you feel the disturbance within the Force. You all do this but most of you do so unconsciously. Pay more attention and use your sentience when "something" feels different, or when other people seem to be acting differently. Of course We all knew full well that some, if not many of the two groups of yourselves, would begin basking in illusions rather than reveling in truth. Long ago by looking forward into the timelessness of the Continuum We glimpsed this possibility taking form. So plans were altered, Soul Contracts were amended and reincarnational periods were shortened *for many of you but NOT for all of you,* in order to have sufficient numbers of Walk-Ins and Star Seeds here at any given moment. The Advocacy Agreement was written to ensure the success of all of Our missions. You walk in great company, you should all be proud of who you are and where you are from. Remember, as I stated before, you do not need to know where you originate from, but IF you do need to know, you will be told. Living with pride in yourselves is what you have learned about you as Soul. It is through heartfelt experiences during your many incarnations to this world and for most of you, many, many other worlds that has made you strong.

An earlier reference I made about all the medical personal and others who are working on your behalf to assist you in the integration process of new Light particles being absorbed into your cellular structure, should be clarified a bit. I heard some fleeting thoughts some of you had that maybe you would be better off off-world working on behalf of those here on Earth. This is not necessarily true. Each one of you has a task, a specific duty to perform. You are all respected for your desire to be here now, to do the physical and Spiritual work necessary to continue the forward momentum of the Golden NOW. Although no one Soul is more important than any other, your tasks demand the most from you as individuals. You now know that this cellular restructuring process is not needed anywhere else other than on Earth and that other Planetizens in other worlds have no need to go through this because they are ONE with all else. Knowing this you should be able to refocus your intents on the lives you are living now. What you do here and now in this moment is what is important. I ask that you remain focused, after you leave this Earthly realm you will have ample opportunities to be of service elsewhere. Many of you will also as your future selves, be assisting the New Earth and the New People in the millennia to come. I realize it is difficult for many of you to understand, but you are still on the front line of defense for the continued survival of the human races. The races that warrant survival that is. Whether you are out in the public eye doing My work or not, each of your contributions to the elevation of the collective consciousness is much needed. Remember, a good idea is only good *if the word gets out so others can take heed.*

OK now, the leagues are strong and in many ways unbreakable. There are always weak links to contend with though, especially with those who cohabit the Earthly realm. This is exactly why I need all of you, whether you are Walk-Ins or Starseeds, to wake up and remember your purpose for this lifetime. You must be unbreakable, you must have the resolve to withstand the ranting and ravings of those lesser evolved than yourself. The leagues will support you in all your efforts; have no doubt about this. "One for all and all for one" are not casually tossed about words. You are the warriors, the teachers, the healers of this time. You have chosen to bravely walk a path that is not always the most popular amongst the masses. Speak your truths when needed and silently bear witness to those who still slumber in the lap of illusion. On September 20th of this year 2013, I initiated Project PUSH to release many of the dark energies that impeded your individual paths. If you paid attention and remember the days following, you will have noticed that something in the Continuum was different. The Continuum was abuzz with excitement as a long awaited event had transpired. One that involved not only you My Children, it involved Light filled Beings from every Universe coming together as one for the common good. Meditate; send yourself back to that day and the days following and you will glimpse the shift that had occurred.

Back in the good old days many of you **may** recall that the idea of a human civilization was exciting and transparently new. Some of you may even recall feeling tantalized by the mere thought of trying something new. A new format, a disguise that would be unique to only you, but consistently diverse and different from any you had worn previously. I ask you now, was it all you had hoped for or was it much more? The Earth Star has collected more than her share of new life forms including the beginnings of a new race of beings. Even in her infant state you and I wandered through the limitless possibilities and you acclimated to many versions of the Creation process. We rearranged other possibilities as a newer better version of thought replaced the old one. We gave to this world the best, the newest of Creations. New lifeforms were birthed; diverse types of fauna were strategically placed not only for appearance, but more so for the benefits that could be derived from the beneficial use of each of these. The earliest Children were taught of their uses and this was passed on generation to generation, extraterrestrial to extraterrestrial. The leagues were strong, unfortunately the attention spans of yesteryear just as they are today, are quite limited among most of My Children who walk beside you. Long lost is the intuit understanding that everything has a purpose, that EVERYTHING is connected in a manner that can not only be scientifically proven, by those who chose to prove it, it can be measured in energetic forms. Any disruption to this process activates the Law of Cause and Effect. Cause is the catalyst for change, effect moderates the outcome. Take for example, global warming... cause and effect. In both the Walk-In and Star Seed groupings you will find that through the process of evolution there are many of your kindred brothers and sisters sounding the alarm bells. They do so to awaken all those who still do not hear frequencies above a first or second dimensional reality. You may feel it is not too late and the effects are reversible and in some instances you are right. In most instances the die is long cast. WHAT HAPPENS FROM HERE ON OUT IS UP TO YOU AND THE REST OF THE COLLECTIVE CONSCIOUSNESS. United for just cause, each of you can come together and mitigate SOME of the effects of the Earth changes underway. "Earth changes" mean that things will never go back to the way they were. Earth changes are necessarily in the midst of the evolvement process of any and all lifeforms inhabiting this world. The planet must evolve, and yes, she too is an extraterrestrial. I bet you never thought about that before now did you?

This world is what you make of it. Collectively WE can assist her as she continues to glide into a higher form, a higher expression of herself. You are the best of the best, which is why you were chosen for this mission that you are on. Remember what I told each of you before you agreed to take part in the *resurrection* of the Earth Star Planet. No mission is mission impossible. You may think you are seemingly limited in your abilities to enact change as an individual, but you are not alone. You are Soul. As Soul you are a very powerful entity. As a collective you are strong, just as being part of your Soul Cluster you are unified. As a Soul in a collective clustering together with All That IS you can do anything. Align your thoughts My Starseed and Walk-In ET's. Stop thinking that you have to do it all alone. Stop thinking that you are better or worse than any other. Stop believing you are not the master of your own destiny. As Masters choose your intents and thoughts carefully. The energetics of your New Light Bodies will enable you to not only be more than you ever thought you may be, your abilities to manifest realties more quickly is at hand. Flirt with thoughts of the future and the possibilities it holds, but **live** in the present. Relax, smile, love and laugh and know that you can do no wrong if you live as ONE, one with Soul and as one with Me. And there are a whole lot of ME's in all of you.

Waves of reinforcements are arriving in increasingly higher numbers at an accelerated pace right now. Those on the Earth Star planet who have given up on believing they can make a difference are stepping aside for others to come in and take over for them. There is no shame in admitting you may not be up to the task at hand, but I ask you to ask yourself one question before you make your final decision. If you do not know if you are up to the mission, how will you know if you do not try? Everyone has qualms; one person could be a farmer in one lifetime, a stonemason in the next. Politicians, scientists, an engineer, a doctor and even homemakers had to go through an apprenticeship to get to where they were good at what they do. You each have worn many Hats throughout your many lifetimes, why should this one be any different? You are Creating here; you are **not** trying to recreate something you or others like you have already done in the past. Recreating is part of the past, Creating anew is the present you and the future you. Think of this world, of your life, as a living

42

room if it helps. All of you have rearranged your living rooms before quite successfully haven't you? That is the most basic example I can give you that *you* can do anything if you first get off the couch and set change into motion. Change is Creation. Be My eyes and ears, Be My hands, My voice, My reassurance. And BE EXTRA-terrestrial Terra-nauts.

In loving service I dedicate this catalyst to all Star Seeds and Walk-Ins who are not falling. Furthermore I dedicate this catalyst to all My *legal aliens everywhere.* Remember ET's when unsure of yourselves ... *ET's call home! God*

Catalyst 3

Influencing the Course of Events

God ... OK now, well we are off to a "rocking good start" so I advise you all to expect this to continue throughout this book. I have no desire to lose any momentum with you; there is far too much to say and too little time to tell you. So it was that when the Advocacy Agreement was initiated, you were then informed that because you each had already chosen your various roles here on the planet, or I had chosen them for you with your consent, that many of you would endure difficulties simply because the dark energies would know one of the pivotal reasons about why your presences were sorely needed here. Regardless of what your individual placements were here on this planet ... in THIS lifetime ... you each still had to live and BE in the right place at the right time. This will explain to many of you Children why you have had to be relocated again and again and again. Those of you who did not have the "relocation experiences" did not have them because it was not necessary. You were each where you were for specific reasons! Also, it was imperative that specific numbers of you **and** certain other Souls who were selected would all leave your indelible thumbprints and footprints in a variety of **<u>specified</u>** areas. I need to make you all aware though that your combined presences were intimidating to the dark, to say the least. The fact that they were aware that literally thousands and thousands more of you would continue to be born into or walk into human form and become the collective consciousness, caused great angst among the dark riders.

This of course was to be expected; it was no secret from them that as a combined force of **mature** and stable Souls, you would eventually be a force to be reckoned with. *And now so you are.* Do not misunderstand the term I used, "mature," it is indicative of you each coming into your own, qualms and all. Your chronological ages have never mattered, what did matter is that you would be ready, willing and able when *the bells tolled*. One of the hazards you have each encountered here is that you have expected too much of yourself while conversely not thinking enough of your own abilities, let alone understanding them. It has long been held to be an Earth Star anomaly that when you Planetizens began to mingle with the millions of Earth Seeds who live illusionary lives, you tend to mimic them regardless of the fact that on a Super Conscious level <u>you know better.</u>

You have all wondered at one point or another in your lives WHY you have been unable to receive the information from Us that would assist your understanding of why you are here and what you are to do. Again and again and again I have had to caution you to await certain "timelines" here before that information was shared with you. I have encouraged EACH of you to FOCUS, FOCUS, FOCUS on your present time, whatever that "present" happened to be. I have done so each time you wondered about yourself and this world. "Patience" is a quality, a type of energy much needed on the Earth Star planet. When you are home you do not need to be concerned about that. At home, because all things exist in organized chaos and all exists in the NOW, patience is not a "commodity" you need cope with, it serves no purpose, it has no value. You simply use your "knowing." But here on the Earth Star planet it IS a necessity. I am not in any way implying that I do not understand your collective impatience. However, just because you have been sent to the schoolhouse planet does not mean that you need to adapt <u>too</u> much to inferior energies. OK, that having been said, this is where your lives to date have experienced so much turmoil. Starseeds return here again and again for the usual reasons besides personal evolution. These reasons are to continue to evolve under harsh circumstances, to find closure with unfinished business they have had in previous lives with other allies, friends, lovers, enemies and to signoff on unfinished experiences. It is also to garner new and better experiences to add to **THE BRIDGE.** I shall explain the bridge in a little while. If you read the previous book, "Beyond the Journey, Life in the Hereafters," you will be completely aware of "The Hats" and how the Hats affect all lives here, in one manner or another. If you have not then I suggest you do so. Many Starseeds in particular have endured much hardship simply because they have not been aware of the Hats and how those wondrous Beings can affect all others.

The Hats, in your present lifetime Starseeds, are still working with you; they do NOT work against you. All of you who are Starseeds have been permitted to have liberality in your choices here. However, that does not mean that your Guides and other off-world mentors have not sent you countless warnings and cautioning signals, as well as quiet kudos when you have earned them. It is through Divine largesse that you have made it this far! OK now, so in this particular life experience you have tested the waters mightily, you have found some contentment in parts of your lives and discontentment in other parts of your lives. Yet you did not know consciously that is, that you were simply awaiting SOMETHING that would give more purpose to your lives. The *bridge* which I spoke of exists as a doorway; one which is a connector between all Universes and exists in ALL dimensions. It is not a grouping of separate bridges, it is ONE. It is but yet another example of the activity of the exponentiality of the nature of the Divine Plan which **you are participating in.** You each have a vested interest in this bridge, just as all Walk-Ins do. The bridge is a perfect tribute to all of you for all that you have ever done and for all that you are about to DO. The bridge contains an aspect of your cumulative Souls; I speak of Walk-Ins and Starseeds alike. As such you should each understand that you are not only representing your own Soul Clusters, but the primary OverSoul as well. Please think about this for a moment and understand the breathtaking importance and significance of what I am sharing with you.

OK, now I wish to address the Walk-Ins' situations and how they impact on everything from the trivial to the ultra-important. Yes, Walk-Ins lest you forget, you too have the Hats working with you. Walk-Ins take heart now; I, just as the Creator and all Others of Divinity here, truly do understand the perilous and yes, very complicated life experiences you each have. It is time for you to ponder your earliest beginnings. You should know that you are in many cases chosen for that role at the moment of your Creation. Although I ask you to please remember this is not true of all Walk-Ins. Each Being who is a Walk-In that has been selected to mature into that role and continue with it until such time the final return to Source has arrived, must play out **more than** duel roles in each life experience. Many of you who were selected from your birthing time spend innumerable life-moments, or for some of you long, long years enacting the essence of your true self on this world. You do so while still working diligently by teaching other newer Walk-Ins residing in the Sacred Chambers off-world. You also work with the Starseed groupings; you teach them how to remember, how to better understand themselves and you provide solace and have deep love for them all. You who are the conscious ones are required to awaken the unconscious Walk-Ins, I speak of those who ARE destined to "remember." Remember please, you are also to function as true role models for Starseeds who in time MAY become Starseed Walk-Ins. You have great responsibility here and I expect each of you to remember this!

If this sounds simple then I must assure you one and all that it is not. Because this pre-selection process is quite technical I will not describe those intimate details. Suffice it to say that We are always looking for specific traits that a Soul has; the brightness of their overall Being and a singular energy which clearly defines an extraordinary Soul. "Extraordinary" means, "One who exhibits a highly advanced radiance from the moment of their inception." It is the beginning of their beginning which ultimately defines their true nature and their true SOURCE. Of course the ultra-blinding Light they emit is a bit of a giveaway too. All other Walk-Ins who have been selected possess different levels of *STAGES* of Soul maturity. They have a defined curiosity about their Walk-In roles and high levels of unstated but visible integrity. You see Children; it must be this way for all Walk-Ins simply because of their difficult role. Although none are better than another, there are those who shine brighter with an extra passion for eternal life. Even they of course must live some if not many life experiences and grow through and with those experiences. Starseeds, it is because the Walk-Ins must enter into a human body and switch identities that their roles are much more difficult than your own.

All Walk-Ins are considered to be Starseeds as well of course because of their true origins. However not all Starseeds are Walk-Ins. But when certain conditions have been met, an established criterion which must be perfectly followed, allows many Starseeds to have the opportunity to transform into the Walk-In role. I will not make public what that criterion is; suffice it to say that this particular metamorphosis is a demanding one, which requires ardent dedication to just cause combined with the ability *to always stand in truth.* Walk-Ins must adhere to this primary concept regardless of the fact that so often they must endure pain or threats of death as part of *the consequences of being right.* OK, the more evolved a Starseed or Walk-In is, the more they are given to do. The more evolved Souls REMEMBER the manifestation and actualization of healing techniques. They must also be involved in teaching others through the use of evolved energies. These are energies which are given to them to use at strategized

48

points in their lives. This is also true of their individual missions. This is why so many of you are called upon to live certain lifestyles rather than be in the public eye. Evolvement is in fact a level to level pace; the more you each expand your awareness and accept the understanding that you are NOT supposed to be a know-it-all on this planet, the easier your thought processing will become. The more you learn from this book the more you will raise your awareness and your work, which are your missions, to a new height.

Because you are each living in this present timeframe, you are gaining "critical-mission experience." I want to deal with some situations you have each been experiencing regardless of your grouping. Millions of you quite literally "feel" uncomfortable here on this planet and at times have developed zero-point tolerance to be among other people here who are just so vastly different from you, that it causes your feelings of alienation to increase. *Look now,* I ask you each to get a grip! No, you are not like those other people nor are they like you. For all intents and purposes, you are each co-habiting this planet and supposedly intermingling whenever it is advisable with the Earthizens as well as with each other. This is but one primary reason why so many Starseeds and Walk-Ins alike either chose to be unconscious of their true natures or I chose this for them. There had been great concern among all of We who are the Luminescents and justifiably so, that too many of you Children would become so enamored with the true nature of yourselves that you would lose FOCUS, become complacent and fail to assist humanity **as you promised you would.** This was explained to each of you in-depth in the Great Hall shortly before you incarnated this time. It was at that point that so many of you agreed that perhaps it would be better if you did NOT consciously remember. Of course though We provided you with a type of "fail-safe" mechanism.

It means that although you would not consciously remember, your Soul Voices were enabled to bring you vague feelings, a distinct sentience of your time IN THE STARS. In your darkest moments here just the feeling that you could draw strength from the stars somehow, has provided an impetus of an inner **knowing** that you are NOT alone! Yet another goodly number of your two groupings asked specifically if they could be permitted to remember. And of course We Ourselves approached quite a number of you and specifically asked you to **have** conscious recall while incarnate. Although there were no actual hesitations from those of you whom We asked, the understanding was definitely there that this could become a major challenge for many of these Souls. *"How to handle knowing so much and yet not being permitted to share all which they knew. How to cope with the lack of understanding and the gross lack of personal responsibility which so many people continually exhibit. How to cope with being "ALONE."* These were the primary thoughts they had; yet We assuaged those shared sentiments quickly. So, *buck up soldier!*

OK now, so many, many of you in both groupings have learned so much more because you have been unconscious of your true identities than you would have otherwise. As to the Starseeds and particularly the Walk-Ins who have remained unconscious even yet today, too many of them have become the very thing they were sent here to defeat! Under the auspices of Universal Law We are required to permit them to remain in their fallen positions until such time *they have had enough of the experience.* That is not to say that their Guides, The Masters and other mentors, both off-world and on, do not continue to assist them. However, even they can only do what they can only do. Their mentors have been "rattling the trees" rather harshly now in an attempt to help them to awaken while they still can. Far too many of these Children however have allowed themselves to become so tainted, so drug-ridden and

50

sexually exploited, that there is no way to tell if there is any space left for their Souls to maneuver into a better position as a means to help themselves.

Everything on the Earth Star planet is so vastly different than it is at home, that it has become too much the norm for many Walk-Ins and Starseeds to try to fit in with Earth Seeds and with others of the two groupings who have also lost their way. Planetizens, all My Children .... This is a prime example of *lives lost*. Throughout the ensuing catalysts of this book I will be explaining much more to you about you. I prefer to maintain a balance especially with this book. So no, I will not simply give you all the information you have been seeking without ALSO sharing information with you about everything that not merely impacts on you, but will also further your growth. I am adamant on that "growth furthering" principal. It is who I am and what I do! I can not interfere of course with the Earth-based desires of the Starseeds and Walk-Ins who have fallen. That would be unthinkable! Those Children have far too willingly joined the scalar masses of the Earth Seeds and are actually content there. I Myself am far beyond the point of continuing to nudge them now. Far too many truly dedicated people here are now forced to work even harder because of the loss of the others. These dedicated people are reaching out even more so now than they did before to help those in the groupings who truly want to be of service. The two groupings should take heart now please; We have been using the contingency plan for this foreseen set of circumstances.

Walk-Ins are now descending at an enormous rate of speed. Much faster than ever before in this planet's history. More and more Starseeds are being born now because their intertwined destinies revolve around participating with the New Earth energies. These ones will also be bringing in more evolved Souls who have CROSSED the bridge. It is true that the fallen have impacted heavily on the planned course of events here and obviously NOT in a good way. Yet, the scales of justice must always be in full sway. So it is that although you who are part of the two groupings have been forced to work much harder than ever before, everything you each do, every thought you have, all your right actions, you're engaging in collective pursuits using pure forms of energy, is bringing this planet to a NEW tipping point. So it is that I implore you each now not to waste your time on lesser energies. This will not be as easy for you all to do as you may want to believe at this moment. Each of you is responsible for continuing to influence the further course of events *HERE AND NOW!* Yes, yes, I hear many of you with rapidly beating hearts now feeling too unsure of how to do this. You simply do it by doing it!

The answer is quite simple; do what you can to influence others. Teach those you can and waste NO time on those you can not. I am going to give Celestial and David a bit of news now ... I had intentionally put this off until now, so they will be the first to hear this. *Publically.* I wanted to catch them off-guard. Celestial and David, I ask you both to spend the next several years devising more and more ways to reach out across this planet and increase the numbers of people who NEED to become part of the Collective Consciousness. Yes, Celest, I know this will not be easy for either of you. OK now, Celest and David you may say what you wish to Me about this ... in public.

Celest ... OH geez, God!! A "heads up" would have been appreciated, you know! Yes, I hear you saying get busy with the Summits and begin some type of worldwide forum for the Collective. God, we really will need some everyday practical help from others in the collective to do this ...*in our spare time!!!* Every time I think we have just caught up with what You ask us to do, its only a few moments or so later that You send us more to do. I am not complaining but sometimes we do feel a little bit dazed.

52

God ... Now Celest, you know I never give anyone more than they can handle. You two are just too darn good at what you do and are infallible in your dedication to service, that I suppose I simply give you more because *I know you can* handle it. Am I off the hook now Celest?

Celest ... I will have to let you know about the hook! God, I have made an executive decision. The first thing I do when I return home when my walk is finished here ... you and I need to sit down and have a long conversation! I need to read the fine print in my contract. But of course I accept whatever you assign me. David can speak for himself.

God ... Thank you Celest for that reply. David, your turn.

David ... Hmm... I have my shoulders back, head held high, and feet steady. I guess you could say I am not too surprised at this, *after all* it has been a little while since you handed us some new project to do... (*David is smiling.*) And yes it is nice to know that the front lines are being replenished. Sometimes even we feel a little overwhelmed with all that we bear witness to and sometimes we ask ourselves if we are doing enough, even though *we know better* than to ask that. On a positive note, we have the springboard you set in motion for us, specifically with the initiation of Project "PUSH." We were pleasantly surprised with the numbers of good Souls from all over the world who came together as ONE unified body/mind and Spirit to participate in PUSH and usher in change. What was truly amazing was the fact they did so while not expecting anything in return. They did so because they could. Another blessing is those who were looking for a means to express themselves, to do what they could but did not know how to do so, are now more confident in themselves and their abilities. And they now know they can do so any time they feel *inspired* to. In times past when we tried similar projects the response was, shall we say, less than enthusiastic. And yes God, although we have already "been there and done that," we can and will proceed with hosting another radio program while being of course our typical controversial selves and sharing what we know to be true. I am sure this time will be on a whole new level and that should be fun!

God, when You ask us to jump we do not ask how high we should jump, we ask You if we are jumping high enough or do You want us to jump higher. And Your response is always, "You will know when you are there." That works for us. We know there is little "time" left to reach out to those who are meant to connect with us. The difficulty always arises time and time again, when we try to find *others of likemind* to share the projects with. That is when we find they are either unwilling or uncomfortable with doing so. It never ceases to amaze me when some people say, "What is in it for me?" I find that typically these lost Souls choose to promote only themselves. On the bright side however, we are now coming into much, much more contact with so many goodhearted Souls from all over this world. They are making a difference and are willing to help out when **the call** is issued. Happily, they did not duck and cover when they received Your Universal sized bulletin board calling for "All Good Souls to Unite NOW!" Some of our best inspirations come while talking with other people who share our truths. I KNOW that You do have a merry way of eavesdropping and chiming in just at the right moments during our countless conversations with people. Count me in, this is why I am here.

God... I will remember what you said this day. I have counted on you in the past and rarely have you let Me down. I ask the two of you to rally the troops, life on Earth is about to become a much more interesting event than it has been. Thank you, David. Now I will continue.

The future NOW moments are not all written in stone. What each of you chooses to do by using your own free expression at any given moment will determine your tomorrows. It is the collective consciousness which will determine at least on a small scale what will occur overall in the immediate period. I ask that you set aside your personal hardships as much as possible and focus on the ever-changing always expansive possibilities for the future that bids you welcome. Today, in the present moment, with clarity of thought and focused intent, you can do many things that may not be possible tomorrow. How is that possible? Tomorrow the necessary components to enact change in the same manner may not be in the same alignment as today. People alter their thought patterns from day to day; planetary and solar events continue to shift what may happen to anyone, in any area, at any time. When windows of opportunities open it is up to you to grasp hold of them with both hands and do what you came here to do. Use your sentience; use that wonderfully Creative, fertile mind I gifted you with. Use your accrued knowledge to reach out and take charge of your destinies. You can positively influence your immediate worlds as well as what you may do professionally. The Children of **tomorrow** will benefit from everything you do if you do things in a positive proactive manner **today**. Think about building blocks that are necessary for any foundations. Many times you can visualize the end result yet you all know far too well that the foundation block has to be strategically placed in order for the other blocks to find their place. Building, Creating, tearing apart the old so the new can present itself are critical keys to tomorrow's tomorrows. The wind can carry a leaf or a seed to an area never before influenced by those particular aspects of nature. A leaf drifts about until its purpose has been fulfilled. Its purpose when it has left the tree or plant is to fertilize. Now imagine a leaf, one which is carrying a seed or pod. See the seed find its way to the ground, this seed then finds its way into more fertile ground which has been enriched by other leaves. The Creative Process has now altered and evolved once again. You are the leaf, you carry

55

the seeds. It is time to uncover them and let nature takes her course and for her to breathe life into them. In Spirit form you drift, you dart, you float, and you glide about, impacting all energetic forms that you come in contact with. See yourself as Spirit; see yourself as the winds of change. For you are this and yet you are more than this.

I know that many of you are filled with fear and doubt of the uncertainty of an unknown future that awaits you. I ask you now to place that insecurity in a place where you can no longer reach it. In order to move forward you must first get out of your own way. We have used the term, *casting your own shadows,* many times in the past. The shadow darkens, the Light illuminates. Turn up your individual Lights and add them to the collective. You are far more than a tiny spark of light, you are brilliant Lights intertwined with the matrix of All that I am. What will it take for you to believe in Me as I believe in you? I sometimes wonder about that. OK, what you are seeking now is more knowledge to assist you in completing your missions and ultimately fulfilling your Soul contracts.

In times past We have out of necessity had to remove you from this world when she underwent major changes. This time is different, this time you are here for the duration. You as awakened Starseeds and Walk-Ins need to be ready to stand tall, and allow others to lean against you when they need to. The Earth changes can not be stopped, nor should you want them to. They can only be tempered or delayed or altered by the collective consciousness of all Planetizens. Terra's body is spinning to a new beat, one she is orchestrating, just as your physical and etheric bodies are to accommodate the new higher frequencies of Light being beamed into you and this world. The Sun and the Moon, as are many other Celestial bodies, are altering the energetics of this world. You must be prepared to ease the distress of other people by offering correct alternatives to what they believe is occurring. You have a unique advantage, you **know** that this world is <u>not</u> coming to an end. You **know** this is a new beginning. The consequences of being right can be a double-edged sword though. If you share too much information with those who are not on your level it will only tend to confuse them or cause them to pull away, so please, choose your words carefully.

I want you to open the taps on the information aquifer in a manner of speaking. For far too long the flow of information has been constrained and regulated so humanity as a whole would be more manageable by those in positions of power. It is time for the truth to stand on its own, as it always was intended to. I ask you to look at the flow of information on this world in the same manner you would a stream or river. Years ago many of the streams and rivers of true knowledge were dammed up to create pockets where the "information" or power, could be released at a rate deemed pertinent to the ones controlling the flow. This altered the natural ebb of the life force of the information, just as if someone had put a chokehold on your spinal cord which would stem your own life-force and limit your mobility. Arteries must be opened the vessels which contains the kundalini of the Creative Process must be allowed to breathe, to flow in a manner that is conducive to sustaining good health. This vessel could be your Earth Mother, it could be yourself, it could be substantiality or even equality and abundance for all lifeforms. It could even be the truth which has been watered down, demonized, or intentionally withheld from the masses. No one can no longer blame anyone or anything for the woes of this world. That drum has played its last beat. It is time to leave the past in the past and acknowledge that mistakes were made on all fronts. Please *teach the individuals* at a pace they can accept comfortably in their minds.

This book is dedicated to all those Walk-Ins and Starseeds who are here now, without all of you the changing of the guard could not possibly take place any time soon. There are other influences which do impact upon this world that deserve a notable mention. For many years there has been an in-pouring of Light particles to this world in order to influence, to nudge, those who were awakening in order for them to remember all that they can. This influx of energy waves is being sent from every Universe by all the Luminescents and their on planet Children. The energy waves which impact you the most right now are as follows: planetary alignments, the Sun's solar rays, as well as the gravitational pulls from wherever the proximity is of the Moon to Earth. As Terra continues on with her movement into her new galaxy, you will notice the varied impacts upon the consciousness of the people of this world. Stars and Star Systems that have never been known of before here on the Earth Star are being *noticed* by those who study the sky. When this first began these people tried to contain the information so as not to alarm anyone. Now the Stars and the Star Systems' presences has become so evident even the people who have tried to deny the existence of these systems can no longer conceal these new beauties. The weather will continue to impact this world. My dear Children, your best tool to open a mind which has been closed, is to use the changing weather patterns as a catalyst. People want to know what is going on. No one can miss these signs for they affect all lifeforms on this planet. Use this to your advantage.

The migratory patterns of the animals have altered as well. Use this information, tie it in with the indigenous populations' prophecies if need be. Remember that a prophecy is not an absolute though. I also ask that you take a moment now and then to thank all those who have come before you, who have given so much to bring this gridline into manifestation. The whales and dolphins, who are your ocean dwelling brothers and sisters, are leaving this world now. They have done all they can, all they were supposed to and it is no longer in their best interest to stay here. The environment has become too polluted. They have been a vast source of Light here on this world. You will have to find ways to balance the scales as these entities continue their transition to their home worlds. Use the gifts you brought with you to find the balance.

The brighter your Light, the brighter your essence becomes and then the bigger the target you will become. Now is not the time to go back into the dichotomies you have labored so hard to eliminate from your lives, from your minds. Remember those feelings of fear, terror, doubt and uncertainty that clouded your judgment in times past. Remember there is no ending TO YOU, only new beginnings ahead for you, for you are all immortals. Separate yourself when necessary from scenes that are not conducive to your wellbeing. Remember that you exude a natural sense of confidence when you come into proximity with other people even if they are not like you, this is completely natural. Use this to your advantage. In other words, use that which is yours, your experiences, your triumphs as well as your failures to express, and to teach your message of the meaning of life to others.

All We do, all you do, has a distinct impact upon personal and planetary events both finite as well as the infinite. However it is you, those of you with your feet on the ground who are Our messengers. (*God is now singing,*) "And the world will be a better place, for you, for Me, wait and see, wait and see."

The Children of this world must be allowed to evolve, this will not be an easy task for any of you to influence. Lofty goals seldom are. However I ask you to remember that the importance of your missions has reached critical mass. Spread the word while there is still time to influence the course of events which humanity as a whole has set into motion.

I dedicate this catalyst to the BRIDGE over troubled waters. *God*

Catalyst 4

On a Collision Course with Reality

God ... Children, although you each have the free expression to choose whatever reality you want to experience here on the Earth Star planet, for many of you it is not until you once again return home that the multifaceted layers of illusions which had covered the various realities dissipate for you. Then truth, REAL truth, is once again known to you all. For instance: if you had decided to experience life as a biker, the type of bikers who delight in behaving badly, there was never a day when you could not have altered that experience and continued on in life living contentedly for the most part, and feeling that you had a purpose in life. Problems always ensue however when a vicarious lifestyle has been chosen and the individual selecting it did not place the, "I only want to live that lifestyle for a <u>brief</u> time," into the Soul Agreement and then forgets WHAT that time span was! Do not for a moment believe that this could not happen to you! Many people have entered into the banking business for instance to see what that lifestyle could offer, of course there was the monetary gain that beckoned to many of them too.

However most of the time when money is seen as power, the people in that profession will not be willing to want to work in a different profession which may give them less status. Yes, it is widely acknowledged now by the two groupings that although money is NOT the root of all evil, it CAN be a precursor for losing touch with the most important FACTS in life. The reason you each have been given carte blanche to "get in touch with the practical you in an unpractical world," was initially to better prepare you for dealing with TRUE life situations. This was supposed to be accomplished by using what you learned through experience and KNOWING what you should NOT be involved with. People who marry for money may have the money they craved but their lives are a sham. Are you aware that regardless of how happy and excited they may appear to be in public they have some of the saddest, loneliest lives I have ever seen? If you understand the true meaning of "collision," you will know that it is a confrontation of sorts, one which easily overlaps and becomes a way of life. No, I am not speaking of automobile accidents; I am speaking of the Children of both groups who have thrown themselves into the "accident lane" of defying their own destinies. While they are doing this they are also harming other people and successfully changing those others' destinies by keeping them all in "groupie" situations. Starseeds and Walk-Ins who are **conscious** of their origins, and work diligently sometimes quietly, in trying to maintain outwardly the status quo which allows them the freedom to be who they are without divulging who they **really** are to "everyday Earthizens," have a difficult way of life, for the most part.

Although they do feel so much safer when in the company of those who are of likemind, there are always many instances of too many of them vying for center stage and exhibiting the know-it-all attitude. No, it is not always because of ego; I want to be very clear about this too of course. Many Starseeds and Walk-Ins have had so much difficulty throughout this lifetime trying to blend-in with Earthizens that they do not honestly realize that they are giving over their personal power to people who do not really care for them anyway. In an ironic twist they are empowering these people who do not care for them. Meanwhile these other people then go on and feed off the energy which the hapless Children are giving to them, thereby boosting their own egos at the cost of the Starseeds and Walk-Ins who are unconsciously contributing to this. It happens all the time; some of you are aware of it and some of you are not. Then of course there is the "insidious factor." This is a plague unto itself. "Insidiosity" is a vacuum which when applied to the human states of consciousness and of course impacting on the unconscious, can and does lay a thin layer of residue in small but steady proportions of a subliminal energy. This energy is quite capable of affecting the minds, the intellects and the INTENTS of Starseeds and Walk-Ins who are NOT grounded in reality. I said, "It is a vacuum" because it is void of Light meter matter. Yet it has the ability to remove the positive energy streamers which We send to all of you, the vacuum then subtly replaces them with these unhealthy, deleterious energy streamers. They can NOT affect the Planetizens here who walk in truth, remain steadfastly dedicated to following the path of truth and are strong in their beliefs, and in their realizations. The exceptions to this are when those of you who ARE Light Workers, FALL. Then, well, all bets are off! Streamers can be of assistance or they can be your worst nightmare come true! The dark streamers are void of life; yet they *feed* off life thereby increasing the circumference of the emptiness. They then transmute the energy of life-force into an all encompassing force of dark matter. OK now, Children, THIS is one major access the dark ones use to enter into the human Spirit!

This then is why you have all been cautioned repeatedly to *"be careful what you think."* Your thoughts can be calling-cards to these types of dark matter. So you see, even though they are a void, the void itself contains illusionary energies compiled by its own collective energies. No, this is not a contradiction in terms! These energies become illusionary when the dark streamers distort the life-force energies a person initially had. They then reach out to other clean people and either collectively or singularly try to recreate the same or similar thoughts and/or circumstances within a person's mind. These types of streamers tend to locate people here by sensing the fears, angers, hatreds and prejudices each person may have. Although it is a void, it does have its own form of instinct rather than sentience. Now be sure you understand "matter" please; in the broadest sense it is seen as the primary material substance of the Universe. In this way matter has mass, it does occupy the continuum of space, and is convertible to energy under special circumstances. Matter does indeed extend itself in space and persists through spatialness. Matter is also contrasted with mind. So what the mind perceives is matter in motion. But if the mind has become polluted with dark streamers it can only see the illusions and loses the reality which Soul struggles to remind you of.

What so many of you here have forgotten about or have little true understanding of, is that dark streamers can be eradicated from your own personal lives. And yes, if and ONLY if, another person who has them and does not know how to rid themselves of the streamers, asks for your assistance you are then permitted per the Advocacy Agreement which works in tandem in these instances with your Soul Contract, to assist another person here in doing this. *IF they ask for help.* The streamers We send to all of you are completely different of course. There is a reserve in the Higher Dimensions which contains an endless pool of highly charged neutronic energies. Although these energies are not electrical in nature, you would consider the energies to have subatomic charges or presences. They exist in what We term "the pool" and the pool itself is highly electrical in nature, but the neutronic charges simply carry those energies. So it is that although they themselves are NOT electrical entities; they carry the charges nonetheless. No, this is not known about here on Earth but this is what they are composed of. They also though do possess a type of umbilical cord; one which is eternally connected with all the stars. This in great measure is what you feel when the energy streamers integrate with your Aura. Your Aura is really your own personal magnetic field, the energy streamers then flow effortlessly and swiftly into your cellular system. Now perhaps you have a better understanding of how all this affects you. *Well, you all wanted new Light bodies, you know!*

OK now, here comes the fine print Children! Light filled energy streamers can be destroyed IF and only IF the preponderance of incoming streamers from another dimension are so dark, so quietly malignant, that a person caught in this circumstance willingly or through manmade coerce-ment capitulates to the dark streamers. In a sense the Light filled streamers suffocate; they can not exist within the mass of dark matter without the individual fighting back against the dark. So once again here is where your free expression comes into play Planetizens. Do you fight to live or do you lose and die an ignoble death? The Advocacy Program has indeed taken all this into consideration for each of you. This is in part why it is of primary importance that you each listen to your Guides, allow yourselves to be led to the greatest teachers I have sent to this planet and LEARN, LEARN, LEARN in order for you each to be successful in your missions. I have been defining your mission to you all and will continue to do so of course in this book. Of all that I could speak about in this particular catalyst, I believe the greatest information I can share with you is to REMIND you that you are each part of the Second Coming. You ARE the Second Coming. You see Children, your individual and collective understanding of the Second Coming has been badly misinterpreted. USUALLY by good people... but not always.

YES, the Jesus THE Christ Consciousness is even as I speak with you gathering more and more momentum as HE and SHE are slowly and intently covering all parts of the Earth Star planet. If you remember in a previous book I took the time to explain to all of you that Mary Magdalene **is the vessel** which holds the Christ Consciousness. Have you forgotten this already? I truly hope not many of you have, but I do see that some of you did. It is because you are each dedicated Planetizens, dedicated to the entirety of this superb and long-awaited Second Coming, which makes you an integral part of Jesus and His Mary. Again I tell you, "you ARE the Second Coming; you hold the vessel Mary in your hearts and Souls and you hold Jesus's Consciousness within the very matrix of your Souls. Indeed Children, you are all so very special. You simply have not been aware of this natural progressive experience. This is the reality of the Second Coming; His Consciousness could not possibly exist on this planet without each of you here walking in mortality while calling Him forth. The more you called to Him and the more you waited with bated breath to unravel the answers to your own questions about the Coming, the closer to Him you became. Today I can not see any separation between you. FINALLY, you are now in fact functioning, living and understanding as united Christ/Mary Beings. YOU ARE ONE! You are ME, you are JESUS and you ARE Mary. In the greatest sense of the wording, you have each been "handpicked" to be ONE with Us All. Repeatedly I and others have been telling you, "*You are the ones you have been waiting for.*" Yet due in great measure to your "blind spot or tunnel vision" you knew naught of what We spoke. Humbleness does have its place in life but to forget any longer that you are the Second Coming would be an egregious violation of all Universal Laws indeed. Let Me see how many of you understand this. Also, you must realize NOW that how you comport yourselves by having this knowledge now will be ONE of the most life defining times of this life experience for each of you. *No pressure, right?*

Starseeds and Walk-Ins - I must have your complete attention now: For too long you have each with few exceptions, been subjected to so much dross, so much misinformation and have experienced so much angst because on a Super Conscious level you KNEW that you were being intentionally lied to, but were unable to find the "truth locaters." Oftentimes in your dreams which are really night visions by the way, and in your meditative states you have been with Jesus, Mary and MySelf... among Others of Divinity. A very few of you actually were able to make the connection between the Beings you saw and the reality of who They really were. Religions had deftly and effectively wiped the Soul memories from your conscious memories. Think about it Children; how would you have lived your lives, how would you have altered your preconceived beliefs if you had known that you are the Second Coming? We OurSelves had to wait, have limitless patience and await the gridline intersection which the Creator defined as the **ONE** essential one for the Consciousness to be unveiled. There was little if any chance that you would have been able to find out about this truth on your own. Too many cards had been stacked against you; the shadow riders and their ilk had too much to lose by allowing you to know the truth.

Then too We must always abide by Universal Laws; We were not permitted until **NOW** to speak with you about YOU. If the times you are now living in were less chaotic, if people were not being shocked out of their complacency as they are now, would _YOU_ have been ready, willing and able to handle this truth, this reality which flies in the face of what you thought you knew? All the experiences you have each had to date have been stepping stones in a sense which you yourselves designed when you were still discarnate. Although I must say that some of you took these experiences of yours to greater heights as well as to lower levels, than you had initially planned to. The end result is that they have made you stronger. Yes, even the painful experiences. Perhaps I should say, "Especially" the painful ones. By no means did I ever encourage any of you to keep on recreating those times. But sometimes many of you did it anyway. Although it was sad to see some Planetizens become jaded, disillusioned and intent on simply existing rather than living, it still had to remain your individual decisions. Collision courses with reality are part of the Second Coming. It is of critical importance that you each understand that these collisions are necessary; otherwise, how would you learn the truth? No, the dark ones are not pleased that you are now receiving this information, nor are they pleased to see that the veil of forgetfulness is rapidly dissipating. However, there is so much power and integrity in the simple phrase, *"the truth shall set you free."*

I do realize that I am sharing much information with all of you that you have not had consciously. However, in all fairness I can tell you that what I call, "small light bulbs flickering" is the best way I can describe to you what I am observing in so many of your minds while you are assimilating this information. To Me, it makes perfect sense that this is occurring. You see Children, your own Soul Clusters are assisting many of you in beginning to feel and have some slight .... remembrances ... of part of the Second Coming realities. Once you have each recovered from any shock occurring as a result of this information, which may seem to some of you to be a bit overwhelming, you will be able to accept the truth of what I have said. This too is where assistance from the Clusters and your own off-world families will prove to be invaluable. OK now, one thing I do not like is that some of you are feeling as though you have had too many experiences that were not good ones, so how can you possibly qualify as members as part of the Second Coming? Starseeds and Walk-Ins alike - walking in human form requires tenacity, strength and the desire to do good and live as a true human being. At NO TIME does it mean that people should never make errors of judgment, it certainly does not mean that everyone should begin acting like Mary Poppins or Peter Pan.

Being human on this planet exposes each of you to the worst of times and to the best of times. Ideally, people should take the memories of what was the worst they had done and the best they had done, and then realize that it is all a part of life here. Surely none of you think that when Jesus walked this plane, this dimension, that He always KNEW the best course of action for Him to take. He was a man, yet He was more than a man. The human aspect of Him required that He too learn to be a part of this world, yet apart from it as well. The God part required that while He was living here and walking with one foot in each world, He had to first and foremost express His Divinity by assisting all the people who went to Him for Spiritual guidance. He had to always have compassion and patience with all people. Yet Jesus had to learn patience here. Jesus did not come here to found any religion. He was here again and again using different names to begin to build the foundation of Spirituality. He was here to be a Way Shower, a very gifted one to be sure, but that did not always cause His stay here to be peaceful. Far from it. Life is about lessons learned through myriad experiences. It is about evolving individually and collectively, yet learning to have compassion for others who are not evolving. It is about walking away when you should and allowing likeminded people to enter your lives when they should. Life can not be lived without having encounters with the Great Inveigler. How you handle those encounters is a great lesson in and of itself. Planetizens, if any of you did not make mistakes, have not had regrets about decisions made or not made, you could not be the Second Coming. The Coming is a grand compilation of fantastic Spiritual energies with Jesus and Mary at the helm. The overall view of the Coming is one which is spectacular to behold in its pristine Super Consciousness and Magna Consciousness states. Throughout all the Universes, ALL Luminescents carefully gathered all molecules of energy that were birthed or Created from the finest energies that the Creator with his own Creation Processing system developed. In this manner He endowed this Omnipotent

Energy by sharing some of His own Creative particles and placing them within each of these molecules. We who are the Luminescents combined all of the molecules I am telling you about and further imbued those with more of the highest, most evolved energies ever Created. Jesus and Mary then proceeded to place a great measure of their own individual and SHARED Consciousnesses within the perfectly formed spherical matrix. This in turn provided the Supreme environment that allowed the endless development of the Jesus THE Christ Consciousness. This development was to coexist in a harmonious fashion within the hearts and minds and of course the Souls, of each Planetizen whether Walk-In or Starseed, who are the Second Coming. This Consciousness does impact on the Super Conscious state. It does so by seeding and sending consistent filtering periods in increments of the Christ Consciousness trickling into that form of Super Consciousness.

OK now, Children; I am doing all I can to explain this process as simply as possible to you. Again however, Earth languages are lax in properly being able to express certain things. The Jesus THE Christ consciousness which you each bear raises vibrations among all of you who are the worthy ones and forces the lower dense energies to be displaced. In a unique fashion it always causes collisions with reality to occur as well. These collisions are most necessary. In your own terms, it is part of the separation of the wheat from the chaff. Do you see? So very often as you each have felt that you "failed" at something, that you each have tried to do so much and yet saw little success in your endeavors, were and are some of the times when you felt that you had failed yourself and others the most. Please pay close attention to what I am about to say: *failures or your perceptions of such were merely dress rehearsals for success.* Get over yourself, OK?

Disorganized chaos causes imbalances to occur in the Earth Star's own continuum. This type of chaos can be traced back NOW to the people who still insist in living frivolous lives at any cost, even if it hurts others. These actions do under the Law of Cause and Effect affect the main Continuum; sometimes it is felt as a small break in the main one. That is not of great concern for she is a self-healing entity; the greatest concern is for the Earth Star's own Continuum. When this one "rocks" or is "shaken" a bit, Planetizens react through unusual emotional states. Tears, depression, sometimes unjustified anger and yes, the experience of "wanting to go home" seems to impact on people greatly. Again however, once you enacted the initial PUSH movement, you set into motion a great collision with reality which millions of people here needed! This too was the initial period when so many fallen Walk-Ins and Starseeds began to "act out" in earnest. They could feel the changes and the changes induced fear. For example: if they each had a "snow globe" and kept it sitting on a desk, never bothering to shake it up, how could they know there was something else to see, to feel, to experience, when all they know is stasis? Part of their acting out now is to try to dissuade conscious Planetizens from STANDING. These Children who once had high hopes of being of assistance here have entrapped themselves in illusions and intensely HATE change. "Change" might affect them, it might alter their lifestyles and heaven forbid, it might wake them up. So, most of them are unconsciously trying to demean you who are the Second Coming. They try to project their illusions towards you. Illusions would tell you that you are not worthy enough, you are not good enough to teach others and that you are ill-prepared to do so anyway. THAT Children, is where one of the greatest collisions is taking place, even as I speak with you. Illusions being cast about this MATTER are manipulated at this time to coincide with you all learning the truth about YOU. Yet, you assisted Us in bringing forth unlimited amounts of new

70

streamers to join the ones you helped bring to the planet during the PUSH phases. Organized chaos is replacing the disorganized ones. No, it will not be an easy time for any of you, but I implore you to hold on to ME, for **I AM the eye of the storm.** You can do no wrong.

You Children who are the true Light Bearers from your own home worlds, as well as from your collective Soul Clusters, are bringing in the greatest, most phenomenal changes this world or any world for that matter has ever seen. Without you, there would not be the catalyst for change that has been desperately needed here. You are the salvation for the human race. Most Earth Seeds will not know immediately why they feel drawn to each of you; they will only know that you have what they need. They just do not know this yet. My Children, it is with the greatest humbleness and respect that I encourage you to go forth and DO what you can to be who you really are. Continue to travel the Light, fill the voids in this world with your love. I can ask very little more of you at this moment, for right now I simply want to tell you that you are who you are and yes, you can be the masters of this world without exercising dominion over others. Patience and perseverance will continue to be your staff and your rod. Humbleness and respect for yourselves and for others will be the gifts you honor yourself with. Others who walk this world that are seeking the way back to Me need your truths. Please, when possible inform them that they need to teach others that none of them lost contact with Me, they just forgot that I was there.

Remember well the void where the dark streamers lie, if you want to know where the false prophets *disguising* themselves as Light Workers came from, this would be a good place to look. Not all false prophets are born that way; many are "groomed" for the position by the dark agenda. You are all waging battles on many levels. You battle with yourself for your sustained connection with your Higher

71

Self. You battle the nuisances and the intentional misdirections being led by the unenlightened ones who busily paint their landscapes of illusions. You battle for Oneness with Soul and the intellect. You battle your desire to feel normal. Has it occurred to you that you are the new normal? You are precious jewels. Yes, some of you are more polished than others, but that does not negate your role of prominence here. The truth is some of the most polished people only <u>appear</u> to be so. The battle for this world was never over property or riches, minerals or position. The greatest battle ever fought as I have told you before is through peoples' minds in order to advance the battle to their hearts and Souls. This is what was foreseen so very long ago. This is why the Advocacy was birthed. This is why you as Walk-Ins and Starseeds are so vitally important to the successful integration of the Christ Consciousness into this Earthly realm. Lest you have forgotten, which I am hopeful you have not, those who dwell in the dark can not create anew, I do believe I can not remind you of this enough. This is Universal Law. They are allowed to only use what is already there. They can manipulate it, twist it and shape it and rename it so it *appears* to be new, but it is only a re-creation. That is why they need the Children of this world to be down and defeated. Even a Child of The Light whose spark is minimal at best can still breathe life into a new Creation. Light is guarded by the truth and taught and instilled in all lifeforms from the moment of conception. This you must teach to the Earth Seeds. When you are able to and with whom you can. To reach them you will need to **Teach the Teachers**, the others of yourselves who have not put all the pieces of the puzzle together yet.

OK, daily lives and routines must be shaken up from time to time otherwise patterns begin to emerge. Patterns are not always a good thing. An example of a good pattern to have though is spending time with yourself. This assists in enabling you to be able to exist in a state of clarity and grace. An example of patterns that must be broken up are routines which left unchecked can not stimulate Spiritual growth. My Children, IF you always know what and where you will be from one moment to the next, how can you hope to be open and be willing to wait for great surprises? Remember though, rigidity in thought, rigidity in beliefs, and rigidity in definitions hold you back. Rigidity, lack of determination and planting your feet in defiance **is you** setting yourself up for a rough time. A bough must be able to bend with the wind, yet not break whenever possible.

Each of you has a difficult road ahead of you in one manner or another. There are millions upon millions of people who have been caught up in lifestyles which are not sustainable and you are the ones that must cope with them. These peoples' similarities of thoughts comprise a large portion of the non-collective consciousness; they are still the mass consciousness. Therefore they have a lower based energy force and illusionary momentum. Sadly their thoughts are rudimentary; they are denser based thought patterns that serve no purpose except to those who chose to continue their existence in a first or second dimensional reality. These two realities are flat; they do not consist of any matter other than the most basic realities and even they are jaundiced. As a person moves into higher dimensional thought patterns the thoughts then begin to have substance. They have patterns which become recognizable, for they can be viewed from all directions. You can not correctly make a diagram of the Universe or the human Soul on a flat piece of paper. It must be viewed objectively from all angles. To those who continue to live lives of repetition, of minimal risk of being confronted by their own selves out of fear of what others may think, if they are not willing to change then they will not in this lifetime succeed at what they had originally intended. UNLESS, you as the teachers, the stewards of infinite wisdom and experience can pry them out of the shell they molded for themselves. Those who think with their hearts are more in touch with their Souls than are those who utilize only the one muscle, which is their intellectual mind. They may have brawn or beauty; however they have no truly unique thoughts. These types of people exist only to mimic others and these same types have the greatest satisfaction when they see others beginning to mimic them as well. Children, I implore each of you who comprise the two groupings I am addressing in this book, to continue to teach these others by living lives of exemplary simple style sans grandeur. Live ordinary lives in extraordinary ways!

You want to know more about how the Earth Seeds were defeated? I shall give you an example, one you may relate to. Imagine a bird. This bird knows how to fly and it goes where it wants and lands upon anything it desires. Now every once in a while it may fly into a window, a plane of glass. Other birds when their magnetic compass is off due to discordant energies from manmade creations fly into walls. From time to time We may see fit to point out to you instances or areas in your lives, present as well as future, that you may be coming into or are presently in, which may cause you some grief or disturbances in your lives. You may refer to them as receiving premonitions; others may discard them as only dreams. Dreams are visions, visions of what has been, what may be, as well as what may be coming. As always please remember that everything is only a possibility, not a probability. Possibilities CAN become probabilities though. Almost everything can be altered to some degree or another. After you read this particular catalyst pay close attention to your dream states. Out of necessity We often have to replay certain aspects of the movie script you each wrote for this current lifetime. In the movie as We have stated before, there are always options to choose in your lifetime. When you awaken from a dream vision after seeing a particular scene being played, try to recall if you altered the event by even a small iota. Each of you Starseeds as well as Walk-Ins have the unique ability to become dream walkers. In the dream state you can alter the reality of upcoming events. You are in essence Creating a new perhaps parallel reality to the one which particular circumstances in your lives had previously aligned you with. Planetary events can not be altered, at least not without massive amounts of help from the collective consciousness. You can alter your destinies to some degree or another however.

One of the main obstacles you have to overcome, and it is not necessarily one of your own making, is to alter the thoughts of the collective consciousness itself. Through Project Push you were able to move, mold and shape energies, whether they were possible thought forms or probable thought forms to alter the course of events. As most planetary citizens are not as awake as you hopefully are at this stage, their combined thought patterns impact heavily upon the world around them. Fear of the economy for example can cause waves of discontent; this can cause angst anger and even jealousy towards those "who have" versus those "who have not." The resulting collision of thought can literally block a person from being able to see clearly. Look at yourself for example; you as a sentient being are doing all you can to make ends meet and at times you still can not seem to do so. Yet others around you seem to do so effortlessly and continue to glide their way through life. Being in awe of what another has can set up a roadblock to your own Spiritual wellbeing. OK now, in a better time, in a not so distant galaxy where Terra is carrying you all to, you will find there will be no need for conversations like this one to occur. There in the future of yourselves collisions between thought and need will be nonexistent. I ask you again as I have asked you before, question everything, question your thoughts, and question the motives of others. Learn to see through the veil and into the void in others' minds, those minds and personalities that haphazardly live egregious lives. They are riding a train to nowhere and the train they are riding on has almost run out of tracks. Be mindful if you find yourself on this particular train that YOU jump off at the next stop.

I must caution each of you, the practical world and Spiritual world are directly in alignment for a head-on collision. The practical world as it has been is no longer sustainable. I am counting on each of you to recognize this and to understand why it is this must be allowed to occur. There are choices each of you, both Walk-Ins as well as Starseeds will be making from this day on which will affect every option which is to follow. With very few exceptions We prefer to leave the choices up to you. However if you are to be instrumental, a KEY if you will, that will open other critical doorways for the elevated consciousness of this world and you are hesitating about making the right choice, We may prod you by removing other lesser value options from you. There are always protocols to follow and the Soul as well as the Soul Cluster is always consulted. Remember, you are not alone, you are ONE yet you are many. It would not be much of a Second Coming if you each had to go it alone, now would it?

I have often heard the silent thoughts of many of My Children thinking to themselves, "In a hundred years none of this will matter." For many of My Earth Seeds who know no better, this is true. They have yet to understand their own importance; however I do expect more from each of you. You are the Second Coming, remember? You carry in the matrix of your Souls *The* Christ Consciousness. You are the Winds of Change. You are on the front line, please be proud you have made it this far. No, the Earth Star Walk is not easy for any of you, but it was not intended to be. I wanted each of you to challenge yourself, to improve yourself. Most importantly, I desired for each of you to believe in yourself and overcome all obstacles. This timeline will never come again. The clock is ticking... make the most of it. And now before I move on to the next segment in this book, I feel it is important for Me to show you what I have had to change. Over the past 18 months I have noticed that too many Children when reading My words would sort of gloss over some words I have used such as when I would say, "I suggest, or, it would be better if, or, perhaps you should, or, perhaps you should not." OK now, I have decided that special force needs to be on some of the words I write. You will see some words such as, "must, or, have to be sure to, or, be sure not to" and so forth. No I am not attempting to give you orders, but I want you all to realize that I have decided to use terms that have a "declaration of force" behind them. It is now My way of trying to be sure you will listen to the words, and understand THE URGENCY behind the terms. Sometimes things must be altered in order to be sure the intent is clear. I do honor your ability to pay attention to detail, and I hope you honor Mine.

I dedicate this catalyst to the realities which birth the New World. *God*

Catalyst 5

Angels with a Cause

God ... OK Children; in this period of learning I do need for you to have a better understanding of the dilemma the Earth Seeds find themselves in. The commonality between their situation and the strange circumstances so many Walk-Ins and Starseeds find themselves in is its own anomaly. In one of My previous books I explained the Angelic realm to you in great detail. However NOW you do need to know more about "Angels with a Cause." Earth Seeds require the same guidance on a Spiritual level which you yourselves do. That is one link between you and them. However, Earth Seeds regardless of the race or culture they belong to, can and do become trapped in a form of "gravity," for lack of a better term. This type of density I am referring to as "gravity," is so heavy, so lacking in any integrity of structure, that it can force bodies and minds to see only the lower dimensional thought waves and prevents people from rising above them. This is the case UNLESS an Earth Seed for example, has decided to force his or her way through it, has made a conscious decision to rise above it and leave the pit of hell behind. This can happen ONLY if the Earth Seeds receive such a jolt to their realities that they intentionally decide to seek better answers and then reach out to find them. These Seeds are of Terra yet it was always intended that they too move into more contiguous levels and degrees of personal evolvement. Obviously because these Seeds are <u>of</u> the Earth, they had a personal responsibility to do all they could do to assist Terra at all times. Then again, so did you. Planetizens, how you each live here on Earth has a direct impact on your own home worlds. For instance; let us say you are from the World Sirius, how you live here on the Earth Star planet throughout your mortality periods, how you love, how you

78

think, and what energies attract you and which repel you will have a direct impact on Sirius. It affects the Hall of Great Records on Sirius, all Worlds have these halls and it affects the higher states of consciousness that the Sirian civilization is always striving to attain or striving to enhance. This is true of all Worlds! It is "cause and effect." "Soul Resonance" is a form of energy which is non-carbon based of course and does not contain "matter" in the accepted form of the term. This Resonance provides and **is** a direct Universal and "home planet" current which links itself to you and yet affects all life on your home planet, whether it is Sirius or another grand World.

So in the case of the Earth Seeds who have birthed into illusions and pander to them throughout their periods of mortality, they recreate the same life situations over and over and over again. Each time they think that they will have different results, and are shocked when they realize that is not the case. Since the very earliest of days here on the Earth Star planet when the shadow riders began to cast their web all over this world, they made sure the web contained the very lowest and densest energies. These were not energies that were here initially. It was the Earth Seeds who were impacted the most ... for a while it was only them. OK, this may be difficult for you to understand, but because of the density here Earth Seeds became trapped in one-dimensional and two-dimensional energies. These dimensionalities simply became stronger and stronger over each ensuing millennia. Life was a harsh existence back then, so the weakest Earth Seeds did not survive for long periods. Meanwhile, while all these things were happening here, all incoming Walk-Ins and Starseeds were subjected to the same density, the same unreal superficial aspects of life. Herein did lay the saving grace though. Children, all of you who are of stellar families, you who traveled here to assist Earth and still had to have the experiences you still needed, have always either consciously or unconsciously felt the stars in the sky seeming to reach out and beckon to you.

Because the very essence of yourselves always felt a bit out of place here, discontented with life as you saw it here on Earth, you were unknowingly holding on tightly to the Soul Resonance cord of life. This too is part of the Advocacy Agreement. I suppose you could say We threw each of you a lifeline. This Resonance is an integral part of each World, each sphere where your stellar families reside. The Resonance falls under the Guardianship of a band of Beings from the Angelic Realm. These Beings have the unique ability to not only guard the Resonance well, but to also enhance this current with Light and Soul matter which exists between a Sirian and Sirius for example. It is in this manner My Planetizens that your stellar families consolidate any type of energy your Soul requires and transfers it in an instantaneous "flash" of Light from your home directly to you. The Angels with a Cause are absolutely tireless in their pursuit of "grounding" the Resonance onto a designated world and INTO a designated Soul. Earth Seeds have every opportunity that you who are The second Coming have, up to a point that is. I have sent so many, many Emissaries here to work with the Earthizens in attempts to break down the barriers existing between these Seeds and the Higher Realms.

However only a small percentage of these men and women have listened, have altered their lives and accepted a prominent role to be Earth Seeds *evolving*. I am truly grateful for each one of these Seeds who has chosen to crossover and fulfill their destinies. Terra had lost so much of what she once had. If all of you, Earth Seeds, Walk-Ins and Starseeds had been able to band together, you could have wrought many miracles indeed with the help of The Angels. OK, throughout every generation of Starseeds and Walk-Ins who have ever been here on Terra, it always seems to be some particular Souls in those two groupings who lack a type of inner fortitude which causes them to cross the line and behave just as the majority of Earth Seeds do. NO, this was **not** part of their pre-birth agreement. But once Souls have incarnated here each one can be damaged by the whims of the personality. As the Angels "ground" the current onto each world which then begins metamorphosing its own structure and begins seeking to align directly with a Soul, it is usually when Starseeds and Walk-Ins experience in earnest the desire to return home. Because Earth Seeds are already home, they can only feel a true attraction to Terra herself. That is not to imply that many of them do not admire the night skies. Starseeds who have entered into an agreement to be born into families who have for so long lost their way, do so for the purpose of not only promoting their own lineage, but to be able ... if possible ... to raise the vibrations of the born-into families and assist them in *locating* a new path to walk. Of course as you all well know, there are many impediments in showing or telling people about a better way to live, about the TRUE way to live.

So it is that while these Angels work with the Resonance current, they are constantly and consistently transmitting more and more information to you THROUGH the current from your stellar families. Obviously Walk-Ins have a more difficult path to tread, even though they too receive the Resonance. When Walk-Ins or Starseeds are unconscious of their true identity, the Resonance held by the Angels feeds them tiny increments of their Soul memories, enough to help them to awaken to their true nature. But again, it is the individual free expression which is the ultimate governing body which allows Soul to awaken or sleep the sleep of the "unknowable." Oftentimes I hear you asking why it is permissible for any of the Seeds or the Walk-Ins to be unconscious of the reality of who they are. This is a multifaceted issue. I will not explore all of it with you now, it would require many, many pages to do so. Some of you decided before you left the higher realms that you could

81

work best without the truth of who you are being revealed to you while you were in human form. Others decided that the challenge of trying to live among Earth Seeds would be better dealt with by them if they remained in a state that would be accepted by Earth Seeds. However, I can not in all honesty say that either of those two plans work well. Then too there is that other big bugaboo, *FEAR*. I have spoken to so many of you Children especially over the last 25 years, reassuring you, showing My love for you and offering you My compassion for your walk "on the wild side."

I have told so many of you, *"your fears are twofold; you fear that you do not have enough, that you are not good enough for them."* Children, with only a few exceptions you have all shared this same fear. Over time I have been delighted to see how many of you have outgrown this fear. The same Angels who are the Angels with a Cause work with all of you both individually and collectively. Yes, they are still attempting to work with all the Earth Seeds they can too. Such sad irony though; it has required catastrophic events and the harsh shaking of realities to get those Seeds from where they have been to where they need to be, if they want to survive here. It is very endearing to Me now though to see and hear various Earth Seeds who are finding themselves in conscious contact with Beings from ancient civilizations, while other Earth Seeds are in-between the worlds of the Realm of the Luminescents and the Earth Star walk. Any further changeover on the parts of other still sleeping Earth Seeds will come to an apex before April of 2015. This is their allotment of time to make the changes. There will not be an extension! Regarding Walk-Ins and Starseeds who continue to fall - you have **far less time** to change than do the Earth Seeds. I and the Angels fully understand that there will be a number of Starseeds and Walk-Ins who will be too afraid NOT to change. No, this is not an admirable stance to take.

Anything you do out of fear will be undone with great rapidity.

So Planetizens, as you feel your sentience, your Soul Voice, the entirety of your Being pleading for your return home, pleading for the peace here you all need so much, I ask that you remember **who you are, why you are here and remember that you are in good company.**

The Angelic Realm while comprised of many diverse factions coexists as one body. There are few exceptions to the rule of thumb, "all for one - one for all." Many from this realm have in times of great need, freely chosen their own selves to incarnate on worlds that were indeed in great peril. Your world was not the only one. Though they rarely make their presence known to the Planetizens they are there to assist, they do on occasion reach out to those individuals who have earned the right to connect with them on a one-on-one basis. OK, since you all know what Angels are supposed to look like with their flowing wings and halos of pure Light they should not be too hard to distinguish, right? Would it surprise you to know that there are many who walk upon Earth now? Would it surprise you to know that many of these angels are the Walk-Ins who have joined forces with other Walk-Ins from other Universes? They do so to help persuade those who have intensely important destinies to fulfill but need to separate themselves from the illusions of mortality. They must do so in order to achieve their goals. Lofty goals require great mentors. The density of this world precludes so many from actually waking up without great assistance.

Although the Angels' cords are tied to their home worlds, their home realms, they too feel the energy which so much of this world emits which suffocates the true Spirit, the true identity of the individual. I am telling you all this so you will think about your importance more intently, a little more in-depth. If you chose to live in the states of fear previously mentioned and continue to believe you are not good enough or not doing enough, an emergency messenger may have to be sent to assist you. Who will this benefit, you? Them? Who gains the most? Is your cause to become enlightened more important than their cause to assist you in doing so? Can you see you each have a job to perform and that each is equally important? I am asking all of you this so you can have a glimpse into the greater picture and realize that you all, Angels as well as Walk-Ins and Starseeds, have been chosen for your particular attributes. Remember the cord, the cord which has been gifted to you as a result of you signing the Advocacy Agreement. But sever the umbilical cords which no longer and perhaps never did, hold any real value or substance to your particular mission here. Unplugging from the world of illusionary matter can be done very easily and you of all citizens on this world should understand the intrinsic value of doing so. The illusionary matter I am referring to is the practical world which hosts all the dilemmas and dramas, fear and insecurities, and attachments that are not good. The angels are helping all people here with this too. ANYTHING THAT IS NOT IN YOUR HIGHEST, MOST EVOLVED, BEST INTEREST, IS WHAT YOU NEED TO DETACH FROM. OK, you can do so energetically and consciously. This is merely an imaginary example now: imagine a cord which has been implanted into your body, one that unites you with a friend or loved one. The cord reacts to the changes the other person has undergone which are not positive then begins to wither and die... almost. You are still receiving energy from this connection. It is in this same manner that the dark energy streamers enter into the void I spoke previously about. This is where the dark infects the wholesomeness, the good qualities each of you have. This is also where the angels arrive to assist in severing the cord. Yes, My dear Children, in time, and considerably more so after April of 2015 has come and gone, the pendulum will begin its steady slow progression to the other side of the scales. No it will not be sudden or jolty. It will be a steady progression. Why will this be? It will be because the Angels with a cause will see to it that no one, no matter which home world they are belong to, will be bereft of any chances or possibilities to improve themselves. There must always be balance in the scales. While the scales need to remain in balance as much as they can be at this time, you yourself need to remain centered; you are the axis point from which the scales swing. Do you understand?

At HOME, *you know*, but here you need to think, examine, question and then respond. It is not any easy place to be for anyone. Although I suspect you have already come into the realization of this. If you want to *know*, to *remember* the true love and feelings of ultimate love, I ask you to look at a newborn child or perhaps one of my animal children at the time of their birth. They are full of wonder, eyes partially closed, yet in awe of all there is. They radiate the innocence, the purity which exists at that moment. If I could harness this energy, these thoughts and feelings that their radiance holds and send them from one person to another person on this world, you would all be catapulting yourselves to the higher realms of enlightenment and being enthralled in every fiber of your Being. The glimpse of this comes through when you take the time to look, to feel, to sense, to BE. This presence or state of clarity also comes when those others who truly love you most send a minute but distinct aspect of themselves to you through the cord which unites you. An extra bonus is that your home worlds as well as all those in your Soul Clusters also benefit from you "taking the time" to allow yourself to BE excited about all the wonders you behold. You can feel the immense love and utter devotion which went into every aspect of the Creation of this Earthly realm and the diversity and uniqueness of all of its lifeforms and yes, that includes each of you. Nothing has ever been left to chance. Free expression is the one exception, for it does not preclude the element of altering your perceptions. The Angelic Realm as well as the rest of Divinity thrives on perfection and perfection survives in a continuous state of flux, of the matrimony with organized chaos and the Creativity of the continuum.

In the beginning when the Advocacy Program was first initiated it was also foreseen that many of you would desire to become a catalyst for change in particular areas where you were not directed to be. Now I am not saying this was a bad thing, I can understand how it is when each of you enters this realm, especially the Walk-Ins among you, who upon incarnating first feel the sense that something is not right and then that they are not on familiar ground any longer. They gaze about in wonderment, searching for something which is recognizable. Then they attempt to become what We have fondly come to term, "the do-good-ers." I understand that the first impulse is to help everyone, anyone who is in need. This is the innocence of you as Soul speaking loudly and clearly. After many disappointments you come to realize that you are not at home and people here do not always believe, respect and cherish all life as you do. This can be quite devastating to each of you. After a time you learn to develop a thicker skin without becoming jaded, while distancing and separating yourself from others who are not like you. All the while though you still reach out and help those who sincerely appreciate your kind unconditional offers of friendship and assistance. OK, where so many of you make mistakes is when you fragment yourselves by spreading yourselves too thin. You reach out in this direction as well as any other direction you see that requires your immediate and complete concentration. You have become a do-good-er and a fixer. Yet too many of you forget the Law of Non-Interference. This too is where the angels enter and assist in the remembrances you need to have. I know that given time if you were permitted you could fix the problems of this world with due diligence and focused effort. Each of you has your areas of expertise chosen by you, or for you, to assist you to help heal Earth well still fulfilling your other planetary destinies. Focus on those please; I am encouraging you to do so. Honor and respect what I am asking of you. Guide and teach those who may be able to influence events in their particular areas of expertise by offering the benefit of your wisdom. Prompt them to spark the flame of remembrance in themselves as well as in others.

Teach others to find the answers themselves, but guide them when they need a helping hand. Later on they will be thanking you for this. If you yourself wish to become better at something, then learn from someone who knows more than you do. If you want to know more about how and why things are, then look, read, learn and assimilate. However, I will remind each of you that the best teacher you have is the inner knowing you have from being in complete unison with you as the personality and with Soul, which is the higher more evolved version of you. I wish you to think about Angels with a Cause for a moment. In time you will come to understand that each of you to some degree or another are fulfilling your missions of moving one step closer to your reunion with Source. Now do not become hasty, this process will take many, many more lifetime to accomplish, so do not get ahead of yourselves. Focus on the moment, this world has already had more than its share of problems from those who have tried to place the cart before the horse. You see how well that went.

As Walk-Ins and Starseeds who are on the path of remembering I encourage you to strengthen the bonds which unite you with your home worlds. I said, "strengthen," **not dwell** upon it. Your home worlds await your return, however right now you are needed here most urgently. Also use the gifts of alchemy you each have. Reinforce and enhance the cords which connect and strengthen the bond between each of you who has chosen to wear the mantle of greatness, by cherishing life for all the wonders life can gift you. Individually you can each accomplish small miracles, collectively with the purest intent, you can shift the tide. The Angelic Realm will be there to assist you when you need it most. Those of you who choose to walk the path of the illuminated will be given carte blanche to continue on Our joint venture. There is no cause which is futile if your intent is pure in its form. Terra's rehabilitation program begins now in earnest.

I dedicate this catalyst first to those Angels with a Cause and secondly to those of you who are Angels in training. *God*

Catalyst 6

Alliances in the NOW

God ... Hello again to all My wonderful Children! You who are all the best of the best NOW radiate more Light than I have ever seen you do in this present mortality period. I am absolutely delighted to see that you are learning more about yourselves than you bargained for when you first started reading this book. At times it requires great courage to find out more about YOU than YOU have ever consciously known before. Now My wish is for you each to arrive at a form of conciliation with yourself ABOUT yourself. You see Children, you are each far greater than you know. You are learning, well learning somewhat, that you do not need to carry this world on your shoulders in order to establish your greatness. Greatness lives within each of you as a staunch, indomitable force of the unity of **ONE.** I truly do understand all the gasps and shock I felt issue from so many, many of your minds when you were being told that you are the Advocates for Justice and you are The Second Coming, just as are Jesus and Mary. Part of the human condition here is to look askance at your own deeds, to find fault with yourselves and to be a bit peevish about what you think of as your loss of memories. Of course if you are **not** being hard on yourselves at some point in your present life, I would have to gasp MySelf and state, *"Look they are finally growing up!"* It pleases all of Us greatly, especially Master Kato and the rest of the Collective of Masters, to bear witness to all your changing thought-forms and your "newly" discovered abilities to be at peace with yourselves. It is not as though you never had these abilities, it was simply that illusionary thoughts and preconditioned beliefs masked them.

I would ask of you each that you quietly give thanks to YOURSELVES for not merely having the desire to format change in your lives, but to actually arrive at the true realization that you are doing what you should be, even if you consider what you are doing to be meager when compared to what others are doing. First thing you do now is ... *stop comparing yourself to anyone else please!* You have your own uniqueness as do others, cherish yourself just as I hope you cherish Me. Remember the Soul Resonance; this current is a tool which you can use consciously. I suggest that all you need do is to visualize how **you** see this energy and then bring that memory into your mind whenever you feel you need or want some extra assistance. Planetizens, the more you practice doing this, the closer to your home world you will be. In the most basic manner of explaining My statement, this is what happens: the more that Soul Resonance grounds itself into the SOULS of yourselves, the more it can enhance the life-cord you bear, while at the same time strengthening the bonding process between each of you and your home worlds. OK, this is a vitally important process which supersedes your conscious self's thought patterns that may be dealing with strictly practical world issues. There is humor present here though; for many, many years many metaphysicians and some of the men and women who have had actual communications with off-world Beings, some of these Beings were Masters, always would speak of a "silver cord" which supposedly united a person with the Higher Realms. They equated it with a type of protection. You see Children, it was not until *NOW TODAY, in this particular moment,* that any Beings have been permitted to come forward and explain that it is really Soul Resonance which they all were trying to speak with you about. However, they had to withhold the true convoluted reality of the cord. So, information which We all would have loved to share with you had of necessity to await, *"The Advocates for Justice,"* <u>protocol statement</u> to occur at a specific spatial period in order for this information event to take place. OK, so it was your individual and collective experiences which

90

gave birth to the protocol statement. One could not exist without the other. This is but one reason why those who have fallen and live capricious lifestyles can not become part of this Agreement. The Advocacy Agreement is very firm on that point. There is far too much at stake for The Agreement to admit anyone into the event who is contentious or has inglorious thought-forms. Yes, I do realize how much responsibility is being placed on your shoulders. But if I can handle it then so can you!

"Advocate" as I define it is, "A true believer in justice, one who promotes the good works of others and those who cluster together to share likeminded thoughts and exchange ideas on how to promote change." So tell Me Children, what is so difficult about that? Planetizens, whatever you are not able to do physically as an Advocate you most certainly can do Spiritually. In fact the latter is the most preferable manner in which to enact change and expand the Advocacy Agreement. As part of your pre-birth Contract when you set your plans into motion to meet and be with certain individuals here on the Earth Star planet, it was understood and agreed upon that when the Agreement gridline intersection arrived, you would be placed in touch with one another by some means, somehow. Each of you long, long ago learned quickly that *the enemy of your enemy is your ally; the friend of your ally is your friend as well.* NOW in this place, on this world, you will be putting that FACT into activated motion, more than even you understand right now. *Alliances made are alliances kept.* Just so it is clearly understood however, those Walk-Ins and Starseeds who have fallen and may have been part of the initial Alliance Agreement you each wrote prior to this lifetime, have had their name energies, their Soul signatures removed from the Great Hall.

We had no other choice; the fallen have not left Us any other proper course of action We could take. No, of course this is not punishment, it is action taken in the name of

91

Just Cause <u>per</u> the Agreement criteria. Please Children, do not stress, fret or needlessly worry about what will befall those other Children. They too knew the rules of Conduct which are relative to the success of the Advocacy. It may require a very long time period for some of them but eventually all of them will come to understand the folly of their ways. It is The Law. This does prove to all of you I hope though, that even if you had your periods of "unknowing" about all of this, you still did not choose to cross the line and become what you are here to change. Of course I am well aware of all the actions you have taken to date that have caused some of you to feel uncomfortable about some of the things you have done in this lifetime. I have mentioned this to you before and I am doing so again in order to penetrate that part of you which shows discontentment and dissatisfaction about yourself for those other experiences. The Soul Resonance current is nonjudgmental of course, all that has dismayed you through the niggling thoughts you have had about your past experiences is fully understood by the Resonance. After all, *you are walking in human form and this is the Earth, you know.* In time, when your present period of mortality has arrived at a climax and it is your turn to return home, you will fully understand that those other less than desirable experiences you have had have made a great impression on your stellar families and stellar allies. The experiences are understood far better at home than you are currently understanding them now. The Resonance cord superimposes itself over each Walk-In and Starseed whether they are in a conscious state of their true existence or still unconscious about it. It is in this manner that small tangibly intangible flickers of Light particles extend themselves out to wherever the two groupings are. This is also true for the small minority of Earth Seeds who are consciously trying to alter their perceptions and are beginning to HEAR and LISTEN to the *voice of truth.*

This superimposition works well with the Beacon of Light Sword. Together they seek and find the "other parts of yourselves" regardless of where each one is living on this planet. Mind links either form or if the formation is already complete, then the "telepathic recognition factor" expands. So it is that while in your dream state you may encounter people you do not know and may not ever meet in the physical that is, yet you remain either consciously or Super Consciously in touch and in tune with them throughout your mortality. OK, this too is vitally important Children; this is in part the Advocacy Agreement weaving its way through your hearts and your minds. Soul already is well aware of all these things occurring and does its best to nudge you to pay attention to what may appear to be random thoughts, random images and leads you to websites for you to visit where you can learn ALL that you need to at any given moment. Obviously when the subject is websites, be careful where you go and use discernment, all right? You have each placed yourselves, OR I placed you geographically where you needed to be for many reasons. Because I need consistency from each of you, your Guides, Master Teachers, the entirety of the Angelic Realm and many other Beloved Beings, have worked tirelessly to assist you in locating one another. Even if friendships with another of yourselves ends, the seeds you each plant and help to germinate in each others' minds continue to grow and bear fruit.

I am going to tell you the simplest way of contacting all others of your groupings. It is so simple many of you Planetizens will wonder why you never thought of it yourselves. The name energies of each other are not as important as are the energy signatures you each bear. I do know that so many of you in both groupings are still struggling with learning how to quiet your minds. Perhaps if you merely focus on a blank wall or hold a picture of a *White Rose* in your mind, you will learn and retrain yourself on focusing. This type of focus is needed. The purpose is for you to learn to keep your mind quiet and remain relaxed but intent on the quietness your mind will learn to feel. Experiment as much as you need to, for I do see many of you already learning that type of self-discipline. All right, some of you are able to call in the others of the Agreement with little effort. Yet for others "of you" this is something so new for you to learn that you may have a few qualms about if you are doing it right or not. Please let go of that insecurity; insecurity is just another name for fear! The ones you call in will be on your Soul levels and stages of Soul maturity and yet MANY of them will be more evolved than you. The ones you call in who are less evolved than you are will have limitless opportunities to learn from and through you. Choose whatever time you want to call, but be sure to <u>issue the call!</u> Simply state to yourselves either verbally or nonverbally, " I (here state your name,) do now call in all others of the groupings who are part of the Advocacy Agreement, who are part of my Alliances in the NOW." There NOW, is that so difficult to do? You can each do this whether soaking in a bathtub; water is a great conductor of Spiritual energies by the way, quietly sitting in a chair, lying on a bed, during a quiet walk, during mediation and so forth. I would suggest you each do this every day, perhaps several times a day until you feel comfortable, until you feel the naturalness of what you are doing. Then decide how often you want to do this. During your rehearsal periods, all those you will connect with will begin to notice some tingling, or at times a slight prickling or tickling sensation may occur. This may happen to you as well. This is sentience responding to what you are practicing and preparing itself to be on call for, it is waiting for the main events to take place.

OK, the very moment you each decide on WHEN to begin the main events sans practice, an awesome energy not unlike the energy of the Creator, will enter your Soul. *And then* **instantaneously** the cord current accompanied by the combined energies of members of your stellar families and Beings from the higher dimensions will connect with the bodies, minds and Souls of the groupings. Everyone will react to this connection in one manner or another. In many countries here the people in the groupings will feel a subtle difference regardless of what practical world issues are assailing them. In some countries the feelings of the groupings will be so strong yet be accompanied with a sense of déjà vu that it will take many people aback for a while. In small increments you will each receive a solidifying energy from your Soul connections with the others that will last throughout your physical life. It is up to you each to monitor your emotions, learn to "read" them. Here are the rest of the steps you need to take; once you have gone ahead and established your Soul connection to the others, then go ahead and call to them again and let them know what it is you want. Your connection is established through the process of issuing your first real call. Think carefully about what it is you want to telepath to the others. Remember though, this is part of the Agreement which clearly states that each Soul reunites with the groupings in order to bring the Advocacy and the Advocates together. This Soul reunion which is indeed an integral part of the Jesus THE Christ Consciousness is to further Create the expansions of the foundation for the Christ Consciousness to use to provide more and more of the sweeping changes which <u>must</u> continue to take place here.

When stating your reasons for this connection, think carefully about what you are going to say. *Keep it simple, but not broad or general.* You may want to write down all your decisions about what to ask, and then read them from the paper while you are asking the others for assistance. Believe Me, the day will soon come when you will all be pleasantly surprised to realize that most of what you each want are the same thought patterns shared by the others. There is what you could consider to be a counterclockwise balance which occurs for people who for health reasons must take prescription medications. This is also true for people who live very stressful lives. This means that they may not always be able to feel the energies which are being sent to them by others. So please Children, I want you to understand that all of you who are in this situation are still sending and receiving whether you are able to know this or not. All right now, when you encounter people physically who are some of the others who are part of the Agreement, do not be too surprised to simply feel a Soul Recognition which may be difficult for you to understand. Regardless if you become "best buddies" or not, you and the others will pass information to one another in many innocuous ways.

No doubt there will be some of you who want to be flagrant when meeting other Advocates. I advise you not to do so. This is not a matter which should be obvious to those who are <u>not</u> Advocates but who may be listening to your verbal conversations. At times you will see that you may encounter another Advocate yet never be verbally or physically in touch with them again. That is fine Children. If the individual destiny is to remain in touch in those ways, then it will happen. Regardless of which it is to be though, I ask you to accept My wisdom in this matter and be content knowing that you are each intermingling with one another within the form of the Super Conscious, however for many of you it will be with the Magna as well. You have many ways of sending telepathic acknowledgements to one another, especially if you feel you will not meet again. My David-Self simply smiles his beautiful smile at them usually accompanied by a slight nod of his head. My Celestial-Self usually gives them an enigmatic smile then nods her head silently chuckling to herself. Their behavior makes sense actually, David loves to interact with all the other Souls *he has been waiting for* while emitting his inner peace and transferring a portion of it to them. Celestial uses her rather offbeat sense of humor when meeting those Souls simply because she is an enigma herself!

OK, now I am going to take the time necessary here and explain, *"The Cross as the tool of Emancipation and interconnectivity."* I have just asked one of these two hardworking Souls who are scribing to insert a portion of a writing they posted on one of their websites a long time ago. I believe you will see the interconnectivity for yourselves. Please read below:

"So, what is the cross? A cross, an ordinary cross: or crosses with crystals, crosses made from metal, wood, silver, gold, whatever materials that crosses can be made from, that do NOT depict an image of Jesus THE Christ on that cross, have a meaning that few have ever imagined. In one of the most malevolent Machiavellian attempts to hide the true identity of a cross, the dark energies continued to impress upon the people the need to wear or have a crucifix with the hope that in this way they could continue to hide a cross "in plain sight." After years of seeding mistruths the Illuminati could not allow the true meaning to surface and have it backfire or boomerang upon themselves. Simply stated, *"The cross is a compass."* The compass denotes North, South, East and West. Each point of the compass represents the races of the world. We are now in a time when North needs to meet South and East needs to meet West, and North, South, East and West need to converge in harmony. In this manner there will be no division between black, white, red and yellow. Some Native prophecies call it the time when the Condor of the South and the Eagle of the North come together as one. What further needs to be understood by the reader, is that the simplicity of the compass is daunting to dark Souls. You see, this means that as a person becomes aware of the powerful magnetic energy that a cross projects to all other people whether they are wearing, or possessing crosses, it enhances and magnifies the Light of each Soul. We ask that you maintain focus and be receptive to understanding that those who wear a cross <u>become</u> a cross. We consider this to be a part of everyone's birthright. No, we are not telling everyone to

97

run out and buy a cross; we want you to at least be aware of the true significance of the cross. As more and more people become aware of this fact, the more these same people can dis-empower dark forces. In this manner more can be accomplished with less effort. Each one of you who understands what we are saying, why we are saying it, and are assimilating the truth of this matter, causes each of you to become a force to be reckoned with. This means that you are moving up another step on your own personal ladder of evolvement and being an active participant "on horseback" with the Golden Now. You are no longer searching for all aspects of your destiny, in many ways you are <u>being</u> your destiny. Remember the cross is NOT religious; it is a Spiritual "direction finder." Each Soul is Its own cross and what a wonderful gift that is! Now that you know what you have and what you are..... use it! And have your Light shine as brightly as the Son of God or the Sun of God, whichever you prefer. From now on you will see simple images of the cross wherever you go, it may be on a uniform, it may be on a road, it can be longitude and latitude symbols to guide you, it can and will be everywhere you go. So just smile and enjoy your gift."

God ... When Celest and David wrote this article it was necessary to continue to refer to all of the races here as, "the four races." This was simply because at that time and until NOW, that was the information you all believed. The gridline intersection for the truth about the races here could not be revealed until NOW. My Celest-Self and My David-Self too must abide by one of the Universal Laws of "Non-Revelation." They can not and will not disclose any information to anyone here UNLESS they are supposed to! So it was that the very same dark beings, who promoted and continues to tout the devious misinformation about all the races of humankind here, did so as part of their *atrocious plan of segregation.* You have all been lied to about the true races since the beginning of linear time here. The Illuminati are not really known for extremely high intelligence, yet their cunning is unequaled. They immediately seized upon the fact that each human Being here will naturally cluster or gravitate towards all other humans **IF** they are allowed the opportunity to do so. It is the natural order of things. The dark ones have long used their "divide and conquer" protocol when attempting to overtake civilizations. Because they can not Create, the dark ones can only recreate, the Earth Star people here were fair game in a torrid, despicable game of the Illuminati which has continued for far too long. All Starseeds and Walk-Ins bear the genetic coding of their stellar families. This in great measure accounts for certain skin colorations here among all races. Earth Seeds have interbred with ALL Starseeds of all nations at one time or another. This is true also of Earth Seeds and Walk-Ins. So it is that each generation of human Beings who has ever been, do in fact carry the genetic coding passed down through their "TRUE family tree," and share the genetics of every Star System. OK now, the great segregation I have been telling you each about was and still is the divide which has caused your country and every country on the planet to be bigoted, callous, hateful, prejudiced and DEADLY towards all countries except their own country and their own culture or nationality. The segregation was to keep all races here in the stupefied state of ignorance which has been here since forever ago. There is not a single race on this planet which does NOT carry the genetic coding of the Star People and of the Earth Seeds. There have been over the millennia perhaps a handful of people who have silently wondered about the Four Races theory. Everyone else accepted the theory at face value; as a result true segregation was born! You have all fallen into the trap that was so carefully built for you. Now if I have your attention; the CROSS truly does symbolize each race of humankind here. It also symbolizes the connectivity of each of you to the other. However, there are hundreds and hundreds of races here, far from the "four" you were raised to believe in.

THE CROSS will assist you one and all with your Soul Resonance and with attracting other Advocates to you. Remember what Celest and David said, "*The cross is a compass.*" Indeed it is; it is a "people compass." No one and nothing shall prevent the cross from fulfilling its mission! I believe it is time for Me to say, "The more you thought you knew, the more you now realize that you did not know very much." For years, Blue Star the Pleiadian, Celest, David and I have been telling you one and all, "*you are all related.*" Yes, I will admit We all spoke in God Code, but really Children, I would have thought some of you would have understood the Code by now. It will be a while yet, but the gridline intersection is rapidly arriving when much to their collective chagrin, the Jewish people will discover that "way back when" Jews did in fact interbreed with other nationalities. **This is true of all of you.** None of you will be able to dismiss that fact! NO, contrary to popular belief, bloodlines do **not** actually become diluted after a certain period of time. People like to believe that though when they discover for example someone in their family 199 years ago who interbred with a person of a "less than desirable race." Less desirable by the family in question that is. The imprint remains within the bloodline however, and that Planetizens is the way it is!

Children, far above and beyond the facts I have been sharing with you is yet another one which definitely also impacts on your stellar races. All the collective of the Luminescents, which obviously includes Me, had so very long ago in Earth time definitions, entered into a Sacred Covenant with One Another regarding the Creation and/or birthing of new forms of life which would be humanoid or would simply be Light Body Beings. The Creator and the Creation Processing system were of immeasurable assistance in defining a criteria for Us to use. The formations of this new combination of related parts could be reorganized and form a new and better whole of itself. As a result it would and did Create a system using hypergenetics DNA and elevated forms of alagorphic geometrical shapes and forms, to birth or Create life forms capable of sustaining themselves on any world. The hypergenetics DNA I speak of are not known about by Earth scientists yet, but eventually on the New Earth they will be. It is a simplified method of combining what you would consider to be genetic materials and carefully infusing them into life forms We foresee coming. This way as soon as a new life form begins to shape itself into a minute Light beam either through birth or the Creation Processing System, the infusion is gently administered to that life form. The genetics here are a combination of ALL of US who are the Luminescents. Our individual genetics are those of the Universe We each oversee. The alagorphic geometrical shapes and forms are a combination of different forms of Light geometry which are necessary for each life form to have. The Sacred Geometry is an intrinsic energy which helps to nourish both the Soul and the genetics. So it is that the Covenant We entered into with One Another became an important part of the foundation of each Soul. Children, this means that essentially you each bear the genetics, the lineage of each of US who are the Luminescents. OK, in the most specific sense possible I want you to understand that all of you Starseeds, Walk-Ins and Earth Seeds, are an aspect of Each of Us, *while still maintaining your own individuality and bearing the seeds of your home worlds.*

You are ONE, yet you are MANY! If the scientists on this planet were yet able to really understand the human vehicle, they would be able to see the countless numbers of microdots which not only are incorporated into the body but are also imprinted within your eternal cellular memory. These dots are the genetics of Our collective of Luminescents; your Souls are well aware of this just as they each KNOW the imprints you bear from your stellar family. You truly are as are WE, *in the company of Gods.* Although We Luminescents do not have physical forms as you understand them to be, We can if We choose to, wear the guise of any humanoid at any time. Although We do prefer Our OWN Light bodies, some events transpire which make it easier to walk upon any world, EARTH FOR EXAMPLE, and be seen as just another person. You each have the ability to do this yourselves. Although with few exceptions most of you walk this type of walk during your dream states. This is all quite relevant to what I am about to say: A decision has been made that between NOW and Christmas Eve of 2014, many of Our collective will be walking on this world. All of Our Children here need a type of reassurance from Us that would be easier to accept if you can feel Our Presences more personally. No, I am not going to tell you how you will recognize Us; that information is on a need-to- know basis, and right now you do not need to know!

I can tell you however that quite a large number of you will be able to FEEL Our Presences, yet will be unable to actually see Us the way you would like to. Some of you will recognize a sensation, a familiarity that is difficult to describe. We will arrive at a certain time in areas which have already been designated as the locations We need to touch. None of Us will be here very long, but it will have an impact on life here as you know it.

OK, here is some news that I would prefer not to have to share, but it is what it is. Because so many, Starseeds AND Walk-Ins have fallen and I can not count upon many Earth Seeds in this particular matter, I need to inform you one and all that Walk-Ins who are conscious will from this nanosecond on have a massive responsibility to assist in saving however many Planetizens here as they can. This is a different aspect of their role here now. This must be accomplished under the Law of Nonintervention; which means they can <u>not</u> and shall <u>not</u> be able to interfere with the destiny of others. However, it is imperative that they form the concentric mind links necessary with all those who are receptive to change, regardless of what grouping they are part of. It is about expanding truth and wisdom now at an accelerated rate more so than ever before. So many cataclysmic events have already occurred here, that as a result many people of each grouping are struggling to rub the sleep out of their eyes and NOW want to know the truth. They are finally awakening BUT for many of them it is too late. No one here can live a life without purpose! There still remain the millions and millions of others of each grouping who simply will not change and that is their choice.

You see Planetizens; this battle for the Souls here is being fought through the mind links. All Starseeds who want to join in this maneuver are most wholeheartedly welcome! No, I am certainly not forgetting about all you can do. I have had to put the impetus on the Walk-Ins simply because they live dual lives here. Obviously this new part of their roles which must be played out now, will not cause their Walk-In status to be any easier and I am sorry about that. Starseeds, please formulate your mind links to include your beautiful thoughts for the soon-to-be completion cycles of the New Earth. Draw a picture, even if you are not artistic it is the image of what you want to convey that is important. Freely use color in the images, for color of course has its own power points. Write a letter to the Universe, write a poem, sing a song of deLight for others to hear telepathically. Starseeds We are counting on each of you to do the right thing for the right reason. Join those you are able to by whatever means are at hand and compare ideas, thoughts and above all you may want to combine energies telepathically. In this manner you will be able to work consciously with the Walk-Ins while still working with the collective of your Starseed nations. The Earth Seeds who now understand what life is really about, those seeds who have managed to break away from the madness and the illusions which have for so long inveigled them into a non-life, are slowly and in most cases taking small steps on the road to their recovery, making a difference for themselves on the path to evolution. These are grand roles you each have Children, I ask you one and all NOT to underestimate the great things you shall accomplish. You see, I believe in you!

OK now, together We can accomplish what many of your predecessors have erroneously considered the impossible. *There truly is no mission that is mission impossible.* United We can Create new mountains on the New Earth, mountains of incredible beauty. These mountains will hold all the goodness, all the wonders and excitement of all We as a collective are trying to achieve here. Reach out to your brothers and sisters, offer a lending hand as only you can do. The time is upon you when you will need one another in ways you are only just beginning to understand. You can supply the Spiritual comfort and understanding so many will be in need of. I encourage you each to cultivate friendships with those who can assist you in fulfilling your missions and in easing the physical hardships you are yet to endure. I am not speaking only of the Spiritual relationships, although you will find as these new found friendships blossom that you will be connecting with each other on a higher level than most Earthizens have previously known. The more you separate yourselves from the mental lassitude so much of humanity has become complacently accustomed to, the sooner the new people will enter your lives. The mental lassitude is now in some cases, beginning to dissipate and subsequently forcing some people to examine themselves. Many of them do not like what they see reflecting back to them in the mirror of self-reflection and self-revelation.

Terra, as she continues her metamorphosis into the new translucent gem she is rapidly becoming, will be assisting you in fulfilling your missions to enlighten the masses of this world by removing elements from human lives which they have become accustomed to and take for granted. She will of course out of necessity need to alter her physical self in ways you are only just beginning to see in order to achieve some of these goals. Each of you will be given information on how to perform tasks which will benefit not only yourself; they will also assist others in the locations you reside in. I encourage each of you Walk-Ins and Starseeds alike to learn to harness the elements, not as masters but as stewards. The elemental forces are your friends; they are to be your salvation in many ways. Terra who is this beautiful and wise Being, knows each of you so very well, all she awaits is for you to come forth and substantiate your desire unequivocally and without any reservations to work with her on common ground. She asks that you consider aligning yourself with the *lei lines* that run everywhere within her surface. No it is not important that you move or relocate to do so. Just state your intent and it will become so. As you infuse these crucial energy veins within her physical being with your own Light Codes you will be assisting her to transmute the dark energies thus enhancing the energetic properties within her matrix. If you feel you do not have time to accomplish all the goals you have set for yourself, I remind you that you can overcome these obstacles by enhancing your abilities to do what you must in the practical, while sending yourself to other locations in the Spiritual sense. In essence you will be bi-Locating, you will be in two places at once.

There are many illusions taking place here. Just because you have to be in close proximity to these energies does not mean you need to become a part of them. Remember you **are** Gods and Goddesses in your own right. If We as Luminescents can expand upon the Creation Process of All That IS by being everywhere all at the same time, then you most certainly have it within you to connect with the life-force of this world to enhance and replenish the grids themselves. You can do this with the grids within this planet as well as the ones surrounding, protecting her. Think about this please when you are assisting in the stabilization of the force fields that cause matter which was Created by THOUGHT to retain form.

In keeping with the theme of this catalyst and continuing to encourage each of you to know more about yourself in order to enhance your own SELVES, I will take a brief moment and remind you of another element of your connection with the others who are not humanoid, who are also here to help balance the scales of justice. Each of you has totems. Totems are animal lifeforms which you have aligned yourself with in the past, as well as here in the present. All animal lifeforms were Created by US and therefore contain genetics which are akin to your own. Their telepathic abilities have never become diluted as they have in so many Earthizens. They live in the NOW each and every moment of their existences, there is no tomorrow and yesterday is no longer a thought. You can learn much from them. You can draw from their strengths as you have done in times past. Their emancipated Spirits as well as their abilities to love unconditionally and their abilities to be community minded should be role models for you all. Even now as I speak with each of you there are new alliances being made within the animal kingdom. This will ensure their survival elsewhere as well as ensuring their continued evolvement into finer expressions of themselves. Each of you at one time or another has felt drawn to certain species, the lion, the tiger, the bear or birds of flight. You feel drawn to the dolphins, porpoises, whales and to the peacocks, the ravens, the hawks and the eagles for a reason. They are related to each of you. Did you know that? Use the strength of this bond to enhance and fortify your resolution to never give up on your quest to evolve, never be content to merely survive. See the beauty in all things while acknowledging that not everything is beautiful. The more you SEE the more you become and the more you enhance that which you SEE, rather than take it for granted. Speak with the Spirit of the water, earth and air. They too are an aspect of you.

As Advocates, per your agreement to BE the Second Coming, each of you must take personal responsibility to maintain your own evolvement as you move through this lifetime. Alliances of the higher magnitude are completed with you as the personality and with you as Soul. Soul knows where you are at any given moment as this pertains to your own evolvement. Soul encourages you to reach for a higher rung on the ladder of evolution. Every once in a while state to yourself very simply that, *"I am now elevating myself to my next level."* Each level has gradients, each level denotes a higher state of awareness. Each level aligns you with new levels of clarity and purpose. Each level builds upon the foundation which is you.

As you now know, each race here on Earth is and was always intended to become one and the same. Perhaps it may be wise for you to continue to learn what you can about "each other." Learn to understand each other's faults and weaknesses and why each is as it is. Use the strengths of each culture to enhance your own self. Most of you have at one time or another incarnated into all the various cultures upon this world to learn from the experience. Gather those strengths, the diversities, and the uniqueness of your cultural and individual Spirits together as one. You are here not to save the human races, but to aid those of the human races who are willing to do the work. You do this by showing them alternatives to the practices and beliefs commonly held which have confined, limited and restricted their Spiritual growth as a collective up to this point. Help them to reclaim their power and rekindle their desire to become more than they are.

I realize it saddens so many of you that you are not receiving the support from your families and friends as you pursue the path to reacquainting your Self with your

Spiritual Higher Self. Under better circumstances this could have been prevented. Honor their decisions by not attempting to interfere and by not allowing them to hold you back. Others will come into your lives that are better suited to growth at this time. I will speak of this again in a later catalyst.

Now I would like to take a brief moment and remind you of other allegiances you have agreed to honor during this current life cycle. Long ago many of you walked with Me on this planet designing, planning and comparing notes about this new world and the Beings who would eventually come into their own. You and I agreed that bonds made would not be broken. To your credit you have tried to continue to do this even though you were putting yourself in harm's way more often than not for doing so. You see My Children, so many of you have come into this lifetime not remembering much if anything at all about your previous incarnations, but with good reasons, I might add. We, you and I, could not allow you to recall something which would cause you distress and quite possibly veer you off course. You may not remember that in times past when the connectivity of all life was *common knowledge,* most of you worked hand in hand with not only the elementals of this world, you also worked those of the Devic kingdom. They need your assistance now, as this world continues to reformat herself into a finer version, as I have stated before. There will of necessity need to be alterations in the landmasses as well as the oceans and river ways. It is these areas where countless lifeforms exist that for many of you are beyond the normal spectrum of the human eye. It was intended to be this way. So as it was foreseen that the world would change and the people would be caught up in the times they were living in, certain factors had to remain just outside their spectrum of knowing. The Devic kingdom's principle job is to restore balance in the microcosmic world, which you may or may not be able to see with a microscope. At times they may be able to be stimulated for a response with use of a laser beam. Rekindle your relationships with these wonderful Beings, I encourage you to become one with them. In your meditations call upon them to come to you and guide you to do what ever it is that they may need assistance with. Right NOW, all of Us need a little help wouldn't you agree?

This lifetime, this changing of the guard here on this world is NOT just about the human race, you all should know this well. This is about the survival of this world. We can always repopulate her later if necessary. Do you understand? Good, now that I still have your complete and undivided attention, be aware that humanity still has no idea of how close they really came to already becoming extinct. Balance and harmony must be attained and then maintained from now on though. As the caretakers of this world you are charged with this responsibility. You do this by properly educating the masses when possible and most importantly you need to find the means to reach the children. Too many children are being lost to the current technological revolution. Technology is disrupting their development. However, in the present NOW teach them through the explanations of technology that technology is just a tool.

Since the subject matter of Star Keepers bears on this current catalyst, I will touch briefly on the Star Keepers' roles in the coming times. Their missions are to assist Terra in her travels; they are to continue to align her physical body into the new galaxy which is being Created at this time. Their missions are also to continue to assist the ground forces, and you are a critical aspect of them. The more each of you can do, you especially Walk-Ins, to educate the other Light workers of this world and cause them to understand that they are here to see to it that ALL THIS which has been allowed to occur here MUST never happen again, is of pivotal importance. The Earth Mother **must never** again pay for humans' life lessons. I am sure you understand this, however I felt it imperative to make mention of this once again. Look to the skies, feel your connection with your home worlds, with MY Self, and with the higher realms. However, right now I need you to focus on what is occurring NOW in the NOW. There will be plenty of time later on to celebrate once the Golden NOW has fully ensconced this Divinely Created, lovingly orchestrated world of Mine.

OK, if you are waiting for the Starships to appear before *you make your move to assist* then you have waited too long. If you are among the many Starseeds or Walk-Ins that may be looking for vindication from all those people who have written you off as being crazy or delusional, then you missed the whole point of the exercise. This lifetime is about you and how you advance in your Soul growth *while* incarnate. This includes but is not limited to how you respond to rejection. Life is not a contest where no prize is given for second place. Need I remind you there are those who walk this world with the sole purpose of testing your resolve? Need I remind you there are those who may appear to wear the guise of a black hat in order to get your attention, while their true identity is hidden under a white hat? There are those who walk among you whose sole purpose is to see if you have really learned what you say you are, or if you are just simply paying lip service. It is easy to fool the average human, the rest of Us are not charmed quite as easily.

I encourage each of you to embrace the roles you have undertaken here. There are those among you who either already have been or are now being placed in positions of power, of influence, they are awaiting the introduction of new ideas. The sign they are waiting for is for you to offer an option, an alternative to the way things have previously been. Use your stellar knowledge and your innate understanding of the basics to unclutter the flow of information. The technology can be presented to restore

110

this world, however first it is the fundamental basics which must be restored to the proper order. Universal laws must be respected and thus taught by you to the people. Light weavers *consciously* contribute to the enhancement of the tapestry of life.

When in doubt about how you are doing or if you are doing enough, ask Terra for guidance and direction. She, like I, knows each of you better than you know yourself. Align with Terra (Earth) herself; **ask her to help you help her**. Extricate yourself from the concrete jungle as often as possible and reconnect with her by sitting in silence on the grass or the sand. Share your energies with her and SEE your radiant thoughts traversing steadily, and speedily through the energy conduits within her matrix, gently touching all the other forms of life, humanoid or not, on this world. Send thoughts of serenity, of tranquility, of enhanced fertility of mind, body and Spirit. And yes, every life form has Spirit, sentience and intelligence. Strengthen your alliances now with the NOW where all exists as ONE!

The alliances you make today will strengthen the resolve of all those whom you will meet in your travels. You see, each of you draws from one another each other's strengths and your abilities to SEE clearly what lies ahead of you. Do not be afraid to say you do not know when someone asks you a question. One of the greatest downfalls of so many Walk-Ins as well as Starseeds is to believe that each of you has all the answers. Humble yourself and be joyful in the knowing that you do not know it all. I wonder how many of you realize that to know it all would ultimately drive each of you into the desire to leave this world and go somewhere else where there was still more to learn. I have heard so many of you throughout your mortality saying out loud or in your thoughts, that you are bored. How can anyone be bored with so much going on all around them is a mystery to Me! In every moment life alters, and for those who say it does not, perhaps they are spending too much time doing nothing of importance, instead of choosing to "LIVE Life." So many Walk-Ins who have arrived within the last 2 years have themselves become caught up in the fascinations of their predecessors' lives. Instead of choosing to progressively move forward and finish all the unfinished business of the previous occupants, they have become enamored by the dramas and practical world delusions. Theirs is a great loss to those of you who continue to be of service and to honor your responsibility to be the caretakers of this world here and now and to do so for the Children of Mine who will follow in your footsteps.

Before I end this version of reacquainting "you with you," I would like each of you to remember that there are those who are close to you in ways you may not be able to fully comprehend. Since few of you consciously recall all you knew before you entered this current lifetime, I understand full well that you can not completely relate to or comprehend life in the Continuum. However distant those memories may be, your greatest teachers have always been the experiences each of you has had. Through mind-link with yourself you may call upon your other selves to unite with you in times of great need. Doing so is as easy as acknowledging to yourself that the compendium of all you are is far greater than you are and together you can push through hurdles that may be stifling your progress in the present. United you stand whole and complete. The silver cord that unites you with your home worlds and into the Angelic Realm also reaches into the matrix of your Souls as I have told you. The cosmic world knows no bounds, there is no such thing as time or distance. There is only oneness, harmony and the poetry of motion that is a symbiotic dance which endures through the element of constant change. If your life alters each and every day, if the plans you made continue to diversify and surge periodically, then you are staying in the flow and are subsequently living in the NOW. Be proud you are being the catalyst for change by **not** having everything in methodical order. So much of organized Chaos is random, it is full of spontaneity. Do not try to predict the future when you have so much riding on the present. Earth is easing her way into position and alignments are being done to ensure she is ready when you arrive sporting your new Light bodies and merging with her new Light body. The age of man is coming to a close, the Alliance is NOW.

I dedicate this catalyst to all those here who are part of truth and wisdom, for truth and wisdom are *the final frontier. God*

Catalyst 7

The Effects of The Trojan Horses

God ... Well everyone, I do hope you are each becoming much more comfortable with not only learning so much about yourselves, but understanding *why you need to know*. I also hope that NOW you can place a greater importance on yourselves and the roles here which you are each engaged in. I do not see any distortions in anyone's energy field due to the amount of new information I am giving to you, I am glad about that. However I have heard a few "gulps," especially from Walk-Ins. These Walk-Ins are the ones who have been so frustrated because they have felt constrained, felt unable to help Create the changes they so eagerly wanted to be part of here. OK, Walk-Ins ... take heed now; remember you can only do what you can only do. This is not a trite statement; it is a realization of a fact which you need to keep in the forefront of your minds. I waver at times between telling you to stop trying to do it all yourselves, or saying, "get over it and simply do what you can." Starseeds are a bit in awe of their own true existence for the most part, they seem to wonder if they are dreaming awake or awake and dreaming. There is a difference you know, you may mull it over if you want to and see what it is. Walk-Ins are in a rather peculiar situation right now. Not many of you Children in any of the groupings are consciously aware that many men and women here who Walk-In are also multiple Walk-Ins. When a pre-birth agreement contains so much work which needs to be accomplished by a Walk-In, it is sometimes necessary for several Walk-In Beings to enter into a designated and agreed upon physical vehicle at different points or arcs in an individual's life here. All right now, I shall use as an example something I briefly spoke with you about in the last catalyst. I explained what Walk-Ins need to do now, remember?

OK then, if for instance a man who has agreed to the Soul exchange was a mathematics teacher then the Walk-In entering would of course would have to be adept at math and remain in that profession for a while. This would continue until a gridline intersection beckoned him to make a major shift in life in order for the Walk-In to move forward and focus on his own personal and planetary mission, then things <u>do</u> change. BUT, this is only true of Walk-Ins who are conscious of who they are. If the entering Walk-In is unconscious of who he or she really is, then it is quite unlikely that that one will be able to achieve a conscious "state of themselves" <u>unless</u> the Walk-In had stipulated in the Soul Contract that he or she would be awakened to their true status WHILE they were wearing mortal guise. *It's complicated.* Suppose a male Starseed who has entered into the Walk-In agreement is a bus driver; at the critical point when the Souls are exchanged, the Walk-In will continue to be a bus driver until he has cleared up the man's obligations which the Walk-In inherited. Then the Walk-In will choose whatever profession <u>he</u> needs to have in order to be successful in his own planetary and interplanetary mission. In other cases however, if a law professor has arrived at his chosen exit point and the Walk-In enters bringing his OWN knowledge of law that the professor would need to continue to have, then the Walk-In will be fine in that role, UNLESS the original professor had planned to go further and make a career change and become an atomic bomb specialist for instance. When the period would unfold as it always does for the professor to start the schooling necessary which would be best suited to his new profession, the Walk-In will immediately exit and just as quickly be replaced by a different Walk-In whose specialties include, but are not limited to the more scientific and physics knowledge needed for that part of his mission. *Meanwhile,* the new

Walk-In must also pursue his OWN destiny while still living the life of the former professor. The new one will remain there as part of the agreement until such time another intersection arrives which signals that the man who was the professor/atomic bomb specialist, is now ready to have a life as an enlightened human being. At that point UNLESS the current Walk-In had signed on to work with people and teach them of the Spirituality all should have, then that Walk-In Walks-Out and a more advanced Walk-In enters. You see? In more complex situations though, a doctor may have had such an unhappy life and wants it to end that he decided that he just wants to "go home." Had he prior to his reincarnation this time also entered into a Walk-In agreement, then he would be replaced just as the other men had been. Now however is when things become a bit tricky for the Walk-Ins. Under the auspices of all Universal Laws each Walk-In MUST complete whatever obligations, duties and responsibilities the one he or she is replacing had. So in the case of the doctor, the Walk-In who was assigned to the man must immediately complete the missions the doctor had and THEN go on to expand the Spirituality of the individual by walking the road less traveled, YET still appearing as the man he replaced. During the "doctor's" road walking, all people who had ever been in contact with him notice great changes in the man, but can not understand what happened. The route most conducive to the evolution of all Walk-In races seems to be to keep as much of a low profile as possible unless the Walk-Ins of necessity must be in the public eye. Regardless of which route is taken by them, the Walk-In must continue to do everything possible to protect his own identity while portraying himself as the doctor for instance, and still appearing to be "normal."

"Normal" in this sense means trying to be the forest and the trees in order to protect their own selves. It is not too unusual for a man or woman who has been replaced by a Walk-In to have perhaps 12 different Wall-Ins enter at

116

different life stages throughout the mortal life of the man or woman. Think of multiple Walk-Ins as teachers on different stages of both maturity and wisdom levels. The multiples that succeed one another do so because the knowledge that one may have is not on the same level that the incoming ones will have. So it is that this line of succession can not be broken UNLESS the Soul of the man or woman who chose to exit decides he or she is now ready to return to the physical vehicle. At that point the Walk-In leaves and the one who was replaced returns. *This VERY, VERY seldom happens though.* I am sure you can understand why! Since the Creation of Walk-Ins began, those few men and women who have chosen to return to their physical vehicles are ill-equipped to deal with this world any better than they had before. Sometimes many lifetimes are required before they truly can cope with this world. Yes, even, many Walk-Ins arrive at the conclusion that perhaps they took on more than they had bargained for. Because of their innate ability to be more than one Being at any given time, they are in the unique but complicated position of being able to touch many lives, many hearts and innumerable Souls. Walk-Ins do not change the allotted lifetime of the ones they replace. When a period of mortality is over, it is over!

On occasion over the last 400 years, Earth Seeds who have entered into the Walk-In agreement have been able to learn much more about themselves than they would have if they had not made the switch. Children, when individuals leave here and are temporarily replaced, the Souls of those who have left are carefully nurtured and protected while they rest in a special realm. This realm allows them to view everything that the "new person" is doing on their behalf. So it is that Earth Seeds or Starseeds can be made aware of the transitions taking place and that alone is enough to cause them to look forward to their future reincarnations. In the best sense of the word they are learning through the Walk-Ins' experiences. And the Walk-

Ins themselves are growing exponentially because they have taken on a more complex, but not easier role in their evolution as individuals. This also strengthens the resolve of the Walk-In collective.

Planetizens, Starseeds also have a tricky path to walk here on the Earth Star planet. Obviously as I am addressing issues concerning the groupings I am only speaking of the Souls who are conscious or semi-conscious of who they are. Although each of you have been Super Consciously awaiting this "timeline" for the Advocacy Agreement to come into its own, you have not always KNOWN what it was you were waiting for. Starseeds share the same "aloneness feeling" that Walk-Ins do here. It is only when you are all suddenly in touch with other "yourselves" that the feeling abates temporarily. But Starseeds, I ask you to please understand that you are not living precarious lives. You may feel that there is so little you can do, but you are incorrect! Life here on this planet would be in total turmoil without you. Just as I cautioned the Walk-Ins I am now also cautioning you; just do what you can do and **be content** with what you do. I feel the matrix of each of you through your sentience, through your Soul Voices and through your heartfelt desires and wishes. I watch your eyes glisten with tears of joy and laughter when suddenly something good happens on this world. I watch your eyes fill with tears of sorrow and disbelief as you empathize with all those others here who suffer the most; those who are not seen for the good people they are. I see your anger at the corruption of the governments, of religions run amuck and of young children being demonized. You do your utmost to remain passionately detached from the madness, that is when you remember to do that, and you do so WHILE either praying or sending telepathic thoughts and images of all that you want to change. *And you think you are doing nothing?* Children, NOW I am addressing you collectively: from time to time when I feel I need to, I will continue to remind you of some things I have told you before. And right NOW, I will again send you some "refresher thoughts." NO ONE on this world was or is expected to solve everything here. It was ALWAYS My intent that you worked together as a conjoined collective. I am not responsible for the heinous goings-on here which so successfully splintered all the races here and ensnared them into enforced segregation.

Spiritual strength lies within the Unity of ONE, yet because you are each an integral part of ONE, you are few, yet you are MANY. I ALWAYS and in ALL-WAYS combine My own thoughts for change and the Spiritual restoration of the human races as a whole with your own. So as you "think" of what you can do and acknowledge to yourself what you are unable to do, I strengthen those thoughts, I strengthen the very foundation of your SoulSelf. If I could only somehow, someway, get you to better understand that *what you think, you Create,* perhaps then you would bring peace to your mind and Soul and simply CREATE through thought the miracles you desire. Yes, Children it does take time for the miracles to come into manifestation, but I assure you one and all ... they do and will continue to do so.

When it is deemed necessary by High Council or by all of We who are the Luminescents, then alternate strategies are set into place in order to render aid to each of you here in the best ways possible. OK now; here is more information that undoubtedly will be new to almost all of you. When the Mother Ship came to the Earth Star planet in October of 2007, all those aboard conducted quiet explorations to all parts of the world. They even took along with them many Walk-Ins and Starseeds from many corners of the world while these explorations were being conducted. It was an astonishing "meeting again and greeting again" for all concerned. All those who arrived in the ship spent countless hours, which in Earth terms would have seemed to be mere minutes, consulting all those they brought aboard from Earth. This was when plans were modified for the future activity of how, when and where Starseeds and Walk-Ins here could better service the human races. We of the Luminescents' collective listened intently as great minds formed and molded great ideas and inspirations. And so a genesis took place with the absolute approval of Us all. This commencement was a beautifully modified schematic which would incorporate Walk-Ins and Starseeds' abilities to integrate with others by the filtering of information throughout this world through **touch and thought**. It would not matter if the other people they would mingle with were Walk-Ins, Starseeds or Earth Seeds. Then by using the advantages which possessing Light offers, they could enter more deeply into the realms where consciousnesses were still sleeping. No, this was not in any way intended to be a case of forcing anyone to awaken, that is just not permitted! However, because Terra was beginning to evolve at a faster pace as she moved forward with her plans for emancipation for herself and those people on the planet willing to remain part of her, the indelible Light Markers, the Light meters you each bear especially since 2007, could assist in turning the tide and helping in the balancing of the scales of justice.

All aboard ship of course knew the Advocacy Agreement would be forthcoming and fully realized that a spatial period had been set into place to allow east to meet west and north to meet south. So it was that a concealed stratagem with the approval of all aboard as well, was initiated and set before all in the Higher Realms for approval. So that I do not confuse anyone though; all Soul Clusters were consulted along with the Angelic Realms, all off-world Star Keepers of course, in other words everyone was brought into this idea of using **One Mind** to ensure the successes of Us all. Each of you who are incarnate here was informed of the newly improved venture. How you were informed was diverse indeed. It was through your Soul Clusters speaking with you during night visions, meditation states and those many periods of a type of quietude which so many of you have when you simply quiet your minds and think of nothing at all. Very few of you will remember this part of the idea; however ever since this was revealed to you, many times you each suddenly feel LIGHThearted or at times a bit spacey, or more commonly you feel a sudden but not understood sense of anticipation about "something" without actually being able to identify what it is. When these feelings occur it is because Soul is rejoicing at the new activity that the Super Conscious is experiencing and dispersing to all Souls, REGARDLESS of whether the people are aware of it or not.

OK, oftentimes throughout the history of the Earth there have been special circumstances surrounding certain events, events which have been catastrophic to specific races, cultures or countries. Some events actually took place but many did not, they are myths. You have all read or heard about the "Trojan Horse;" granted it was a myth BUT the concept of the Horse was about a concealed stratagem. Ironically, even today many people here use that concept as a means of exacting influence on other people or on other countries. Unless a maneuver is for the betterment of a country, culture or race however, it should not be used. Although in years past the Trojan Horse was admired by many people in different countries because of the simplicity of the idea, it was not long before different branches of militaries in many of this world's countries built their war games which are actually training sessions, around the concept of the Trojan Horse. So, in 2007 an adaptation of the Trojan Horse came into a manifested FORM of a different aspect of the concept. This new, better, more refined and certainly non-deadly form of the concept is the one that I have placed into affirmative action in late July of 2009. It was necessary to await that particular timeline because of the massive chaos that was unfolding here as a direct result of much of what occurred in 2008.

The adaptation process was a great enabler; it was one that all Planetizens as well as the small numbers of Earth Seeds who would begin to change could all participate in. The affirmative action I spoke of that occurred in 09, was when We added to the Advocacy Agreement what We term, *"The Effects of the Trojan Horses."* There were many Souls in 09 that were in distress because of the fear and anxiety attacks that the personalities of the individuals were experiencing. That in and of itself was a major turning point for much of humanity however. I do not like to see shocks permeating the minds of the people here; yet it is in sadness that I have observed this happening repeatedly. It is in sadness that I see that at times it has required great shocks to occur before many people finally and at times reluctantly wake up. No, of course I had nothing to do with what happened in 08 as far as the shocks are concerned. I and others had forewarned you one and all that it would be necessary for all things to change here that MUST be changed. It was inevitable that this would all come to pass. Too much darkness which had been brought into this world had been self-perpetuating, especially for the last 27 years. That 27 year time period was when We witnessed humanity as a whole becoming absolutely ballistic, completely out of control and more deadly than before. This then Children, in 2009 was when I sent the Brigade here. The Light Brigade that I sent to Earth had a specific mission to fulfill. This Brigade was composed of many of the most evolved discarnate Souls ever to join together and descend here ALL AT ONE TIME. Their combined missions were to sweep over this world as a monad of organized chaos and reach deeply into the darkest minds of the unilluminated people here. That was the cause; the effect was that because this much amassed Light was entering into dark places with a swelling of limitless highly evolved energy, it was in a way piercingly painful to the minds of those individuals. Please remember what My Celestial-Self has stated in the past, *"Light always casts forth the shadows, but it is the shadows that define the Light."* The shadows definitely defined the Light especially in those times, because the Light itself brought by the contingent caused massive disruptions emotionally and mentally to the dark minds inhabiting this Earth. If you think back to that year, you will remember many instances when turmoil seemed to be the only thing you heard about. People everywhere became afraid of what would happen next; even though the media would not disclose to the public all that was happening, it was the people here themselves who used all means to communicate with one another, regardless of the geographic distances. THIS was how so many of you learned more about the rampant madness that other people were displaying.

The Brigade was here for as long as they needed to be. When their missions were completed they immediately beamed off this world and returned to their own realms. The results of their good works are still to be seen still now as more and more of the dark-minded people continue to fall. You may not hear about it all, but I assure you it is happening! OK, in 09 after the Advocacy Agreement had received the addendum I spoke of, was when all of you who are the Advocates began receiving countless telepathic messages from MySelf, the Angels, your Guides and Master Teachers and Others in the Divine Realms. Most of you began to awaken in the mornings feeling more tired than you were before you went to sleep. That was quite understandable, it is still happening today, you know. It was necessary that We ALL communicated with each Advocate and gave each of you all the information regarding this part of your journey. Most of you Planetizens and the few Earth Seeds who were changing began altering your diet; bodies were requiring more of some substances and less of others. There was and still is an intensity of **thought** that seems to surround you each because it is part of your electromagnetic system. A merging has taken place there too. This then is when We unveiled, "The Effects of the Trojan Horses" to you. Some of you may remember a bit of this, but the majority of you are not yet conscious of it.

This Divine Plan merely required you to be told now about what you can continue to do on this, the last leg of the great changes this world desperately needs. What We told you and showed you through imagings and forms of advanced Sacred Geometry, is that you would be kept in certain locations until the need for your services compelled you to be relocated, or you could even begin working in a different place. There are many of you who MUST remain geographically where you are as far as your living arrangements are concerned. However, here is where various changes performed by you will take place regardless of where you live or where you work. I need to speak with you a bit about Light in order for you to better understand the advanced role you are each to play now. Light is its own constitution; it travels in an arc shape when it is regenerating itself or when it is drawing more currents of Light waves into, through and then away from the main part which is the centrifugal force of itself. The more currents it draws to itself the more it can project not only outwardly in short bursts, but in all directions in huge swaths with or without a catalyst to assist the force generated by the incoming currents. All right, that having been said, I remind you that you are each composed primarily of electricity, not water as you have been told. So it is that Light attracts Light and the Light then in your case serves to fortify your electromagnetic system while enhancing your various stages and levels of consciousness. Those of you who are to remain in specific geographic areas rather than be relocated, have as great a duty now to perform as do those of you We still need to relocate. You should all already have the understanding that you can send Light just as you can send love to all parts of this world, to all parts of this Universe. Some of you do so through thought, imagings and even songs. Others simply focus their concentration on the term "Light," and imagine it sending itself to all corners of this world. There is no one method to use that is better than another, **BUT**, now you will be able to do something you have all wanted to do, but you can now do so on a grand scale!

Children, this is such an exciting time for you, all the experiences you have had and all that you have been in training for as the true Advocates is now opening doors that would otherwise remain closed. By now I would expect that some of you have been receiving small glimmers of understanding that you are the Trojan Horses. Think carefully about what I just stated please. By using this strategy you are in a good placement all over this planet. To be the Horses in human guises which would cause you to be seen as ordinary people allows you to now perform extraordinary feats. I suppose you could consider this to be bringing mythology to an upgraded but TRUE stance in life. No longer is it a "fable," instead it is a way of combating the dark people and dark places here, but doing so without violence. Under no circumstances should you resort to violence unless it is to defend your own life. You can not change another's consciousness or peoples' beliefs through violence. If you have to resort to violence then you have already lost! OK, now that you realize that you are part of an enormous undertaking here, it is advisable for you to learn to use Light and *be* Light in a more expansive manner and yet be the Trojan Horses that you are. Light is not a static energy; it is malleable; it possesses a flexibility that lies within your bodies and works independently away from your minds, UNLESS you are willing to work with it and to harvest its power. POWER in this sense is not an aphrodisiac which mesmerizes people; it does not cause them to become entrapped in the illusions which pseudo power projects. Light is a substance that you bring with you during each incarnation yes, but if it is not consciously used in all instances of life, then you are not receiving the benefits you were intended to have.

Planetizens, I ask you not to focus your minds on the question of how much Light you have. Light does beget Light you know, so regardless of how little you think you have or how much you would like to have, it is important that you understand you can not <u>force</u> Light to expand. It does so by itself using its own consciousness to determine how much Light you have now, how much you may need and how much you can handle. I will tell that now you can call Light to you, but do so with the understanding that I am **not** speaking of the Light you already have. Light itself exists in an endless "reserve" of macrocosmic Light matter and does indeed contain all the different prisms of luminescence that exist throughout all parts of the Higher Realms. So Children, all you need do is either verbally or nonverbally say, *"I call to myself the Light of all Lights and ask you to expand yourself and enter into me and work through me."* Yes, it is this simple, BUT you MUST remember the wording, THAT is very important! No, it is not complicated so please do not make it so. The best times to call in the Light is when you are either alone and without any distractions, or with a group of others who are like you and want to participate as a group. Obviously, this is not to be shared with people who are not changing and could care less about changing. If they are not Advocates they do not need to know about this! By calling the Light to enter into you and through you it Creates almost instantly a direct connection from the Light reserve into and through you as you requested. Yes, this type of Light effort IS yet another part of The Jesus THE Christ Consciousness. It is then at that crucial juncture when Light enters you that this Light will mold small areas of itself and spread out throughout the physical vehicle while enhancing the Light you already have.

Once the Light enters into you it will not leave until you are ready to make a final transition from this world. You only need to call the Light in one time, but if you want to simply practice the procedure a few times, you may do so.

So it will be that when you have finished **issuing the call** you will be ready, willing and most able to use the Light THROUGH yourself in order to affect changes here and leave your special Light signature wherever you go. The effects you will have on everything you touch will surprise you, once you realize that this works and is simple for you to use. You can go to a store, a park, a theatre or for a long quiet walk and still spread the Light from yourselves into everything you touch. It could be a shelf in a store, a park bench, a flower, a piece of clothing, an animal etc. It will impact on everyone and everything in that area, especially upon those who are in direct physical contact with where you touched. Use your originality please; think about areas that you know about or think need a Light infusion, or animals that can benefit from it. In hospitals or doctors' offices and so forth you can touch a piece of furniture, a magazine or whatever else you feel can benefit. If you work in the medical field, touching a patient's chart for instance will spread the Light, thereby causing amounts of darkness to suffocate. If you do not work outside of the home, then think of everything you can shed Light on: mailboxes, a neighbor's tree etc. Do not forget to touch the outside of your house if you want to move!! Remember that while you are being the Light it will also cause other people to benefit from your telepathic thoughts. Do not attempt to force another person to change though, that would defeat this process! If there are people you care about and they are good people but perhaps still not awake, you can still share your Light through telepathy, but do so in those cases with no expectations. The Light telepathic thoughts you send will take root in time, and that is all you need to know about that circumstance.

You should use the key words, "I AM the Light," nonverbally while you are using the sense of physical touch or telepathy to alter conditions. No, it is not necessary to think the key words each time you are using Light to alter conditions. I do see though that many of you will try to use the key words simply because it makes you feel good and that is fine too. Some of you may feel tired when you first start using the Light; it is because your bodies and your own Light cells are adapting to a higher state of consciousness and you are evolving. There is no mystery about any of this; it simply was not time for you to know before. Everything you touch will not only respond to your "touch signature," everything you think also will. Children, the simplicity of these effects you will each leave, will indeed have long-lasting AFFECTS which will successfully impact on this world. Planetizens in every corner of the planet can use these effects regardless of what level of Light they are sharing. It is quite necessary for the Light to have different gradients OF itself, but function THROUGH you in order to be able to touch all life forms here. If you think this sounds too simple, then I suggest that perhaps you have spent too much time analyzing different things in life, thereby becoming caught in needless and detrimental "complications." It is your touch signatures which will be dispersing large quantities of Light; it is your Light-filled thoughts which will work with the signatures. This is why you, as the true Advocates for Justice will always be remembered for what you are doing here. Once you **fully integrate** with this massive Light infusion of a different nature, you will feel quite ordinary as you continue to use your touch and thoughts. This is to be expected, you know. All integration with new matter and new energies do in fact settle down and simply flow once the integration takes place. Actually, I prefer it to be this way anyway. I really do not want to see all of you leaping around as if you just stuck your fingers into a LIGHT socket! I am already seeing enough of that as you have been reading this book.

Before I continue I would like to encourage you to maintain your continued involvement with all of your Spirit Guides and for those of you who have made contact already with your Master Teachers, I ask you to reinforce your bonds with them as well. This you should consider to

128

be *mission critical* at this time. They are semi-patiently waiting for you to reach out to them. The veil has been lifted; so this reunion of sorts will benefit not only you, more importantly these Beings can guide you on how and when to remember the effects of the TROJAN HORSES. Although they are always with you, imagine what you could accomplish by being ONE simply by periodically acknowledging to them and to yourselves that you **are** **ONE**! The road ahead may be paved with golden Light; however it is also littered with many obstacles with the sole purpose to impede your progress. And there has been up to this point too much interference; so it is time for you to become more activated and to use the Light in ways many of you are still lacking knowledge of. Light like Oxygen is a great cleanser. Use the Light to free up the energy particles which Create oxygen. You can achieve this through thought; do so individually as well as with others of likemind. So much of this world is dying due to excessive pollution and waste particles being callously disposed of in the waters and in the air, as well as upon the land itself. The more the plant life deteriorates, the greater loss of life there will be. Send the Light to areas which need it the most. Be expansive in your thoughts. Those of you who are adept at this process, please focus your intents by using your thoughts first. Then you may visualize the transference of Light particles by seeing yourselves sending the transfers of Light to areas which you see are in need of the infusions the most. Another aspect of using the Light to enhance and stimulate your own growth as well as removing any obstacles which stand in your way, is to use the Light to clear away any emotional debris that may dissuade you from fulfilling your personal needs. Focus your minds before you attempt to do anything. Send the light through all forms of communications, thereby ensuring there will be no interruptions as well as no negativity coming back through lines of communication channels. When speaking with Us use the Light to make sure you have a clear channel. If you feel you are not receiving clearly, simply send more Light. As I told you earlier there is an unlimited amount of Light for you to draw from. Use your Creatively fertile minds to enhance and expand upon your consciousness. As you do, you will notice many changes occurring for you.

Your periods of manifestation will enter more quickly and your understanding of what is transpiring all around you will become instantaneous. Always be aware of your surroundings and use common sense in all that you do. You will not fail yourselves. This fact is common knowledge off-planet, keep everything simple and revert back to the basics when you feel the need to. Each one of you sitting comfortably in your own space with a clear heart and an inseparable connection with your indomitable Self working unobstructedly as Soul, can soothingly churn a stagnate pool of energy. All matter, all life is energy, but of course you know that. Working behind the scenes, you can in the Spiritual sense affect changes which will trickle down into the practical world where so many Children solely exist. Tiny, steady amounts of Light focused into the darkness will begin to illuminate this planet more and more and thus remove or expose the dark. Evidence of this is occurring in rapid succession everywhere at this time and it will continue to do so at an accelerated pace with your dedication to BE-ing of service. You are the new wave paving the way for the New People who will be Creating the New Earth. Call upon MySelf, and call upon My Jesus and Mary Selves when you feel worn down or unsure of which direction to take next. Your Guides and Master Teachers will be right there with you, along with My Star Keeper Children and all who reside on your home worlds are cheering you on. There is a massive collective working on your behalf. However, it is you who think that you are few in numbers and are incarnate at this time who must initiate then CONTINUE with the changes. And it is YOU who must Issue the Call when you need assistance. I made you each a promise long ago to be there for you during times of sorrow as well as times of joy, nothing has changed since then. Promises made are Promises kept! But you all know this; now you need to continue WHEN POSSIBLE to refresh the memories in those Planetizens who still wander aimlessly.

OK now, not to confuse anyone who is still contemplating what I said earlier about multiple Walk-Ins entering into a physical body, I would like to add that it is not always necessary for this to occur for someone to alter their profession. Each of you is quite capable of learning more about anything you see as a new experience you would like to try. Chances are you already know what it is you are being drawn to learn or experience, you just have not *at this time* remembered what you know. It is times like this when many of you, both Starseeds as well as Walk-Ins, will choose to indulge in "refresher courses." These will occur during your dream states and down times. *Down times* mean when you are having the feeling of **Being** more off-planet than you are feeling you are Be-ing in the physical world, during a particular period of a day. Each of you can also petition your "family" for the option to go to "Night School." This will in some cases be honored, if We feel it would be beneficial for you to do so without interfering with lessons yet to be learned. And as long as it does not conflict with your abilities to successfully complete your primary missions at any given point, as well as overall fulfilling your destinies. The reason I say "might," is because many Earth Walkers become distracted or narrow-mindedly focused or preoccupied with what *they believe* they may be in need of. Thus they miss out on other more opportune moments which may have already been set in motion for them to experience per their Soul agreements. In this manner it is not a case of not being able to see the forest for the trees, but being unable to see the tree which lies in the forest of opportunities.

You My dear ones, as true *Advocates for Justice* bring an entirely new meaning to the expression "hiding in plain sight." As you are MY Jesus's Second Coming cleverly disguised in your Trojan Horse attires, you should each feel proud of being not only capable but ready to embark upon missions of this magnitude. Now you should no longer feel the need to wait for the signs of the times heralding great change, you are the SIGN and you are NOW in the Times, and you are My heralds. It just doesn't get any better than that. Expose the lies and deceptions and reveal the Truth for all to see and then let Truth STAND on its own. Once you begin to defend your truths they lose all validity, I have cautioned you all about this before. If you do not understand what I just said, then please take as much *spatial* periods as necessary to understand. Thought energetically attracts like or similar thought patterns and truth is not merely a thought, it is the all encompassing elemental force of All That IS.

Please remember that those who are still entrapped in the illusionary world here may not have yet noticed that the rug of complacency and indolence is being pulled out from beneath their feet. It is your presence that is aiding this long needed removal because you can now define your presence, whereas prior to now your understanding was much less than it is today. So it is that the continuous infusions of Light and change show markedly through your indelible fingerprints and are now more so than ever before enhancing the Light We bring into this world. This is strengthening the bonds you are making with this world for the betterment of all concerned, far more than any of you realize. You are able to do this because you are on this planet defining your presence and being doggedly persistent in your determination to bring in a better way of life here and *because you can*. The effects you each have on this planet are incomparable, yet you know it not! Most of you are working behind the scenes nonchalantly yet at the same time optimistically, working from within the system that is in total disarray. You are aiding in the total dismantling of the old way and strengthening the new way for new civilizations.

Are you now beginning to have a greater understanding of all that each of you can do? Do you have a better grasp of who you are yet? Do you understand what you are capable of doing with thought alone? Are you now beginning to understand, to *remember* what Light is and all you are capable of accomplishing by harnessing these two awesomely Creative powers?

OK, it bears mentioning here that you all need to refresh your memories of how to better work with your physical vehicles. These bodies are really not limited in many ways, even though they must respond to certain physical alignments or physical disabilities. As long as good health is present they are quite capable of enduring many hardships while taking you safely and efficiently through any task you have to do throughout the duration of your stay here on this world. Each Soul who has ever incarnated into a physical body is quite capable of working with their bodies to activate certain minute changes when necessary. I spoke about this before in one of My earlier books when I explained to each of you in great detail about **the mirrors** and your ability to change your appearance by your perceptions of yourselves. As each of you as maturing Souls continues to evolve you will find you also have the ability to alter other aspects of your physical being. You can do so in order to better integrate with the ever-changing, sometimes erratic environmental changes plaguing this world at this time. It is not always necessary to know why or how changes occur, it is necessary though that you learn that only YOU CAN correct or desensitize them as they occur. Density and gravity must be respected and considered at all times, for each affects your mobility and motor functions. Respect your bodies and they will take care of you to the best of their ability. All Beings are capable of aligning with the delicate flow of energies as these energies merge throughout the bodies. However, it is only those who truly believe in themselves and understand their abilities that are capable of doing so in most instances. You have the knowledge, it is up to you, it is your responsibility to do so in order to heal or remedy what ails you if it is still possible to do so. In some cases physical problems can be so tenacious that it can not happen.

During the earlier years of the 70's, 80's and 90's Walk-Ins and Starseeds set the stage and prepared the scene for the Advent of the Advocacy Agreement. This set the pace for all Advocates to study and learn about what was acceptable here and what was not. This was an agreed upon step up geared towards enabling all of you Advocates to bear the effects of the Trojan Horses. The Advocacy Agreement clearly states that all the Advocates' forces were to unite with one another and do so through love, compassion and most importantly mutual understanding of what you can undo and what you can not. Are you better understanding why over the years certain events which have occurred have defined those timelines and initiated the successive birthing of the following years? These were events that were meant to happen and have happened in order for positive change to be enacted. Think about so many events you knew about please. See if you can follow the trail of what the end results were. If one is not aware of what, how and most importantly why, something occurred then they can be blinded to the truth and to the consequences or beneficial results of any event. Now, since many events were life-altering catalysts for change, I ask you once again to look back over the years and see if you can distinguish when there were events which occurred which were of malicious intent and which of those were catalysts for the expulsion of disorganized chaos as a means to allow organized chaos to enter into the Earth Star realm. Were they of a Spiritual nature, were they energetic changes much needed here on Earth? Or were

134

they meant to keep minds in a stasis type of mode? Many times it was for the sole purpose of giving the masses a chance to see that not all which occurs on this planet is how it was intended to be, nor was it how they themselves would prefer to see it IF they had more control over the course of events which defined human history. I am telling you all this simply because it is when a Starseed or a Walk-In makes their move and become the emphasis-point for awareness which can not be defied, denied or found to be irrefutable, that is when those of you who came to do so much actually did go ahead and "made your move." Each of you adheres to the Universal Law of Cause and Effect. So it is that when you cause something to bring in change to the continuum, you affect change and your EFFECTS become part of the permanent solution. At that point it is not up to you to determine the outcome, you planted the seeds and you today and still others tomorrow will have the passion to continue on with what you each initially began. You see, after the initial event was birthed first by thought and then introduced into the physical realm it became truth-walking. Now that you know more about yourself perhaps you will stop feeling as if you are but a small flickering Light in the vastness of darkness and begin to realize you ARE The Light that is calling and beckoning to others to come join you, as well as to *PUSH* the darkness further away.

Over the years, especially in the last few years, I have borne witness to many of you who aspired to be more like someone else, someone you may feel knows more than you do, or is better at remembering. This particularly applies to those of you who were chosen or have yourselves chosen to share Our words of encouragement and to inform those who have yet to activate their telepathic abilities. Please try to remember that every one of you on Earth no matter how similar anyone's levels of evolution may appear to be, are still on different levels and stages of personal and planetary evolution. I have tried in the past to make it clear that in order to reach everyone on this world it had been decided that information must be shared on a level of understanding applicable to the level of awareness the intended receiver is on. Please remember this as well, when you share information with another whether it is through verbal communication, or through the written word, once the information is received and "Understood" then the next time an individual revisits the information they will be viewing the same words but on a whole new level of consciousness. In this manner they will gain more from the encounter. This is why I encourage each of you to reread what I have said throughout these books. Do not try to memorize them that would be counterproductive and downright impossible. Your best course of action is to take all I have "reminded" you of and compile this information with all else you know. Then you can continue to Create new thoughts and new ideas emphasized by what you already know. Creation is not static; it must be allowed to remain in a constant state of change. Even if someone tried to stop change now, it could not happen. Once a thought is birthed and spoken of or written about it will be revisited and that in and of itself is the catalyst for change as the thought modifies itself. Those who adamantly refuse to change or to evolve, inadvertently have the opposite effect on others. The others I speak of are the ones who want change, want to evolve and walk away from those that do not.

One of your biggest assets is what you know and that you each as My cleverly disguised Trojan horses, can and should work with the parents of young children when you can. Teach them not only how to protect themselves from physical as well as psyche attacks, teach them how to teach their children as well. In this manner the parents themselves do not become the weak links. It can happen if the parents are not able to see clearly that they must remain centered at all times and to be able to trust that their children are able to tend to themselves psychically.

Another aspect of your missions is to offer people a second chance to believe in themselves. Nearly everyone who has ever had a physical incarnation has at some point or another during their time on Earth needed someone to lean on and someone to set them on the right course. What they do with what you offer them, is up to them, NOT TO YOU!

OK, there are many of you who due to your strategic positioning will be in far better positions to reduce or eliminate certain orchestrated events initiated by those who still cling to their power bases. Also, many of you will have the responsibility to not only see clearly what is about to occur, even more so you will be in a position to offer diversionary tactics. This will be a way to support a positive proactive movement which will benefit everyone, rather than the evolvement of only the few, it can be the evolvement of the many.

Others of your groupings are there to promote not only your own good works, but to promote the good works of others as well. This is very important, the time of segregation must cease now. In essence you must come together as one to fulfill your Advocacy Agreement. You need each other now more than at any other time in Earth's history. In this manner *one by one*, becomes *two by two* and exponentially blossoms into "one for all and all for one." The concept of one for all and all for one was not a human strategy; it has been this way since the dawn of the Creation. In other words it did not begin here nor will it end here, understand?

I dedicate this catalyst to all the effects the Trojan Horses will Create. *God*

Catalyst 8

Wounded Warriors

God ... OK Children, now is the time that I must speak of other matters, but these matters are ones that do indeed impact on each Advocate. Many Advocates are experiencing great distress because they can not convince or even talk to their own children, other relatives or even longtime friends about what truth is. They can not get the other people to understand that those people are being badly duped by self-serving people and the unilluminated minds on this planet. I truly sympathize with all of you who experience this. I am so sorry that I can not rip the veils of "needed" or "wanted" illusions from their eyes. But I can not do what I can not do. Those who need to have the illusions can not seem to be able to survive here without them, at least not until they CHOOSE to learn that the "need" itself is but an illusion. Then there are the ones I am speaking of who "want" the illusions, they crave them because the "want" has become an addiction, they believe they can not live without them. These people, friends, relatives, lovers or even former spouses can not be helped by you, unless they contact you and ask for the help. This is where some of the deepest, most painfully emotional hurts ensue for you who are the Advocates. I can not give you percentages that would be understandable simply because they are always in a state of flux. But I can tell you that even though there may be people you love who ask for your help, who say they really want to know the truth, well, not very many of them will maintain either that desire or actually follow-through with altering their current beliefs. That part requires work and a willingness to become part of the truth rather than to settle for a life less well-lived.

However, trying to convince those you love that they are incorrect is a gesture in futility. So many of you are suffering such great heartache and such deep sorrow, but foolishly place blame on yourselves. You do so simply because your minds become spastic because you can do nothing for them. They will not allow you to. So, My Planetizens, I ask you, which is the greater measure of incorrectness here? Is it for you to continue to try to change what you can not? Is it the loved ones who feel you may be daft and experiencing flights of fancy because you tell them or try to, about things they do not want to hear? Is it because it is so difficult for you to simply allow them their freedom of expression without interfering with it? I know of course the correct assessment here; however it is for you to be the ones who answer those questions for yourselves, please. Those questions are one side of the coin. Here is the other side: In order for those others to actually be able to SOME DAY arrive at the correct conclusions about the trueness of life and what it means to each of them planetary-wise and inter-planetary-wise, they and only THEY can cause these unfortunate and unhealthy experiences and their beliefs as well as their chosen lifestyles to come to a final conclusion.

Because you love so deeply and want so intensely to have these beloved ones succeed, you tend to lose your focus because you are too close to the situations. Passionate detachment simply means for you to use certain actions to honor those who are either falling or never even gave themselves a chance to move forward. The honoring of their choices is accomplished by you, by your accepting the right actions necessary and placing emotional distance between you and them. They chose the illusionary life, you should consider how their actions and reactions to you and to the Greater Truth lowers your energies then infiltrates your feelings causing you to feel that you are being alienated from them. It is like an infectious disease; one which I strongly advise you all to distance yourselves from! Do not think for a nanosecond that it is not contagious; it does indeed cause other good people to fall, over and over

139

again. I feel your outrage because these people prefer to link together with others who share their own mind-thoughts, their own perceptions of which lifestyles are best and basically care less about very much else. Planetizens, I must caution you now, when you begin to feel that anger, those major disappointments with them, *then you are becoming part of their own chosen dramas!* That is extremely unhealthy for you and will essentially harm your self-confidence; it will cause you to feel that you are struggling against the wind. PLEASE, stop this! Although it is well-known throughout this entire Universe that I am NOT above dropping some "bricks" on My Children's heads if I feel it will ultimately help them, I assure you I will not interfere if you choose to be a drama-king or drama-queen.

The majority of Walk-Ins who are Advocates face a different type of dilemma. If the man or woman they are replacing had a family, children, or parents still living when the Walk-In exchange took place, life becomes a bit too interesting for these Walk-Ins. The unconscious Walk-Ins do seem to struggle for a while, while they are trying to remember where they are and how they got here. Although the majority of all Walk-Ins do have a tendency to change their diets rather radically at times, in part they are experimenting and then deciding what suits them best, regardless of what their predecessors enjoyed. Also it is the unconscious ones who have a sense of bewilderment until a certain timeline arrives for them and IF they are destined to be conscious of their true identities. It is not uncommon to see them being pushed aside by the family units they have joined. Nor is it uncommon for Me to hear their families whispering that mom or dad is really strange! Sometimes these Beings feel that they are square pegs being placed in round holes. This slightly amnesiac state will last for as long as it will last. It is different for each unconscious Walk-In. OK, for those among them who do have an important mission to fulfill here, strategies are set into place long before they arrive on this planet about how, when and where *specific* events will take place that will cause their "bell" to ring and awaken them. This Children, is where I have at times needed to use "bricks!" *Whatever it takes.*

All contingency plans are set into place to allow the Walk-Ins to enter as painlessly as possible. Of course the manner of their arrivals here are usually painful for a while. Their reception here by others who are not Walk-Ins or Starseeds can be a bit of a conundrum as well. As part of the failsafe system that is provided for Walk-Ins, it had been agreed that they would encounter other Walk-Ins here at specified periods. Each Walk-In will spend time with other Walk-Ins and the more evolved ones will work with the lesser evolved ones. This however does not preclude the fact that many of the most evolved Walk-Ins will be placed in touch with other Walk-Ins who are on the same Soul level and Soul maturity. There are always Walk-Ins waiting in the queue for the agreed upon signal that alerts them that their help is now required to assist struggling Walk-Ins. Then too Walk-Ins always locate certain Starseeds or are located by the Starseeds themselves who are ready, willing and able to align with them and together work for Just Cause. It is part of what is known as, *"The Illumination of Light."* Simply stated this is part of a major cornerstone, a larger part of the foundation of true life that all Starseeds and Walk-Ins share as they join together. All destinies are preplanned I suppose you could say. It does not mean that anyone's free expression can not alter the course of their destiny, but the groupings being conjoined here on the Earth Star planet strengthens the bonds they shared on their home worlds and also enhances the Resonance Cord. This is a major part of how the Creation Processing System continuously works to ensure successes here and aids in removing energy distortions whenever possible. Starseeds are also able to remember <u>certain</u> aspects of themselves, IF and WHEN they choose to. If a strategy had been set into place by the Starseed that had been part of his or her pre-birth agreement, one that had a type of governing communicator allowing certain memories to surface or one that was restraining those memories for a specific period, then whether or not the memories would surface was already determined and would be difficult to change. It is not uncommon for a Starseed to encounter a Walk-In and immediately know the other person is a Walk-In, even if the Walk-In is unconscious of his or her true identity. Starseeds are delighted to work with the Walk-Ins and help them to remember who they are and why they are here. Few Starseeds can explain, "How do I know what I know," to anyone. Many Starseeds and the most evolved Walk-Ins do have a "knowing" and they always have difficulty trying to explain this to others. They usually reply when asked HOW they know about so much they say, *"I just know!"* I must say I do chuckle to MySelf every time this occurs. I do understand their frustration with not being able to communicate to others HOW they know, which of course causes them to stand out like a sore thumb among other people, but they are being entirely truthful. Also, there are Beings among the groupings that finally become tired of answering that question and simply say, "My intuition tells me." Amazingly, people will accept that better, especially people who are clueless about what intuition is. *Strange but true.*

I am addressing all of you now regardless of your identities: stop grieving about the things you can not change; celebrate and rejoice about the things you can change, all right? You did not travel so far and leave your stellar families behind, to fail yourselves now! The more you expand your individual and collective consciousness, the greater Light you always emit. And it is that very Light which either draws others to you or repels others causing them to only want to keep their distance from you. Please do not become concerned about all those others who want nothing to do with you. You could consider it a complement, you know. It means, *you are doing everything right whether you know it or not.* Part of the great difficulty you have each had to contend with besides a lamentable lack of self-confidence, is that inherently you have the greatest desire to trust everyone. You want to connect with everyone so you can share truth and flow with one another rather than grow apart from one another. I am sorry, but it has just never been possible on this planet to do these things and to simply be allowed by the ones avoiding you, to just **BE.** These tumultuous times you are each living in are a clear indicator to you of how much you are needed here. Or it should be! Much has always been said about "suffering the slings and arrows of dark minds." **I** suggest that it would be far, far better for you one and all to instead think of every success you have had to date in this lifetime. It matters naught whether it is small or large, success is still success. Unfortunately too many of you try to measure your success by using your mind as a yardstick for the measuring process. That is really not an acceptable way to do that. Success is acknowledged by the SOUL; and SOUL has no need of a yardstick. Stop trying so hard to do what should come naturally! OK, Planetizens, each experience you have had shields from your mind's view the next great challenge awaiting you. Soul understands this and is always prepared to expect the expected and the unexpected at any given moment. The more you each release your preconceived understandings about success, the more successes you will have.

Speaking of which, now that you are learning so very, very much more about yourselves do you not consider **the fact** that you are the Advocates for Justice to be a superior success story in its own right? *I do!* The greatest concern We here have for all of Our Advocates, is that some of you will not allow old wounds to heal. That is NOT right action on your parts. True it is not all of you who are doing this, but still there are far too many of you still refusing to let go. All that can do is cause damage to the psyche. Needless to say you all should know enough about what happens when psyches are irreparably damaged. Again and again I have sought to reassure you one and all that you truly are not only part of the solution you <u>are</u> the solution. Tell Me My Children, is that not enough for you? Are you fully prepared now to leave the past where it belongs and satiate your hunger for knowledge of the "future" by BEING the future? My Jesus Son has been spending so very much time with you not only collectively but individually as well, you need to know this. His form sweeps through the planet bringing unlimited understanding of all you each have endured. He touches people and all other lifeforms and each blade of grass on his journey. He has been breathing life into many animal species in order for them to continue to have life and fulfill their final Soul Contracts here. He is honoring their requests.

When He touches each of you His touch is always gentle and at times many of you feel that a beautiful warm Light-filled breeze is brushing against you. As part of the agreement with each Soul Contract, He is spending much time visiting those of you who have been ill as well as those among you who are preparing to make a transition from this Earth world. His love, just as all of Ours is unconditionally yours. He shares with you His wondrous gift of laughter that seems to many people to sound like a faint musical scale at a distance, yet can be heard close by as well. It is well-known that He touches a person's hair and shares an imprint of HimSelf through the touch. Yes, of course people who are bald feel His touch as well. He sings to the babes and they laugh when they see Him because they CAN see Him and of course they know who He is. There is nary a single Advocate who does not have time spent with Jesus. Do you believe He would do all this if He did not care so much for you who are the other parts of the Jesus The Christ Consciousness? Of course He knows who you each are! Jesus and Mary Magdalene assisted in the selection of all Advocates. The Planetizens who were here long ago were the ones who were in great part responsible for setting the pace, elongating the road less traveled and as the "pioneers" they truly were, chose to return here again NOW and walk among you. Do you really believe that you have lost so much in life? Do you really believe that We would not always be here for you? We are here, there and everywhere for you all, *because We can be and because it is part of right action to protect all those whom We love - and to love without imposing conditions on love and love you all eternally.* Is that not enough for you to know?

Children the more dedicated you are while you are in service here, the greater the tests will now become. No, I do not test you and I am not speaking of you testing yourselves. Now that I have divulged the long held secret of your Advocacy Agreement and of you as The Christ Consciousness, those very sources of dark matter, of darker minds, will KNOW that YOU know who you are. It has long been understood by them that the timing of when the tide would change here would depend on you. They knew it would be when you realized who you are, thus releasing the power you hold in your hearts and minds. Obviously I fully expect you each to respect the power that you have. The realization of all that you are and all you can do IS power! This power is part of the final battle between all that is material and all that is Spiritual. The material world was built on power-play and power-ploy principalities of thought. The Spiritual world Created so very, very long ago was and always will be the purveyor of all of the vast collective of Spiritual wisdom and knowledge, it will always remain as an immense matrix of the Creation Processing. It is not a contest between these two worlds. Although it had originally been intended that each world could coexist with the other and use special technologies for the betterment of Terra and the Children here while still enhancing all human races living Spiritual lives, it could not be accomplished. Too much intentional interference and hatred of Spirituality developed instead. That was then, this is NOW.

OK, anytime you seem to feel that you are having some difficulty remembering little things, or perhaps a thought starts to form in your minds but you suddenly forget what you wanted to say, do not fret about it. As your physical vehicle is making alterations to itself, other changes are also taking place. It is the formation of new matter that is not gray matter but Light matter and it is infusing your minds. As the NOW accelerates its pace here, it is common practice for the mind and Light matter to be in a bit of a fluff at times. Your mind, Soul and bodies are trying to keep up with living in the NOW. Remember, everything in the NOW happens simultaneously, so but of course there is a new retraining process taking place. This will also impact on many peoples' eyes here as the eyes are trying to adapt to a new vibration and altered frequencies of Light. No, you are not losing your minds as these things happen, in a way your minds, the thinking processes, are being rather gently pushed aside in order to make room for the incoming energies. This is why as the muted or dark energies attempt to cause you to feel less confident about yourselves or unsure of your roles here, that you must remain strong. The time of the greatest **STAND** has arrived NOW. As you assimilate all that I am telling you, if you feel unsure of yourself for any reason, simply think to yourself, "I AM the Christ Consciousness." Those words possess some of the greatest Spiritual energies you will ever know! Also remember to "Know your enemy," and Planetizens, the enemy is still the unilluminated minds which are being fed anger, hatred and misinformation. Everything you have endured in this life experience will hold you in good stead for the present and future NOW periods for the rest of your mortality. When you are ready to I suggest you take a few moments, I said "moments," I do not want you to overdo this experience, and see how what you have gone through in this life has prepared you to be Spirituality invincible NOW.

From now on and at times it may happen when you least expect it to, you may find sudden inspirations, new thoughts of how to accomplish whatever you need to. You will think of or receive suggestions of how to connect with others who are also exploring new and better ways to formulate thoughts. I advise you to practice using imagery and to project images to others. This is all part of the Creation Process; write a letter to yourself if it will help you and list all the thoughts you may have of how to send out to people the Spiritual energies needed that you as the Advocates feel can be of assistance. Be specific please! Remember *what you think you Create.* You are each entering into a period of grand manifestation; please use it well. The first step to your final recovery from being the Wounded Warriors is to stand-fast in your beliefs, more so than you **ever had** before. The second step is to expand upon everything you are learning in this book by seeing how beautifully all these truths blend into all of your consciousnesses. When you are accepting all this consciously your Super Consciousness will raise you up to another higher level of consciousness. The final step is simply, "go forth and live your truths." I ask no more of you than this at this moment. Eventually, you will each arrive at the true conclusion that as a collective as well as individually, you are power personified in the name of God.

As a collective, as a force to be reckoned with, I am sending you some needed instructions. Combine your present thoughts with the new thoughts you are having so that you are Creating a newer thought pattern. Revel in your newfound awareness of all that you are. There are many miracles you will be able to perform in this lifetime, and no I am not encouraging each of you to learn to walk upon water. You can do so much more than that to astonish yourselves as well as to assist in the process of freeing the minds of others who are like you. Are you going to go forth and spread your Light and allow your minds to soar with the benevolent feelings you each will have? This would result in the strengthening of your ties with all of Us though your Resonance Cord. Or will you choose to be bystanders, bearing witness to what others are doing? Whichever you choose please know that it is ok; as long as you keep your forward momentum in motion, then you are doing what you came here to do. Oftentimes it may be the barest flexing of your Spiritual muscles, the very minimum effort that you put forth because this is what you agreed upon initially and that is all right too. Remember what I told you so very, very long ago: "this lifetime is about you and all you could accomplish through dedication and devotion to Spirit." I also informed each of you that it would be this one lifetime which would shine above all others with your quest to finally sever your connections with the physical realm and strive forward in search of loftier goals. In this lifetime and only this lifetime, we have made certain provisions for each of you to be able to work through any karmic debts you may have. Do you remember this? Are you doing everything you can to take advantage of this in the here and NOW? Children, the more you work though your emotional states of unrest while leaving and severing your ties with the past, the faster you climb the rungs of the ladder of successes made manifest and the farther you will each go in this lifetime. For the first time those of you who MAY have any karma that needs to be settled, now have the opportunity to release all your karmic debt in this one lifetime. In so doing you will be not only entering into a new phase of life you will be easing your way into the future lifetime which awaits you. Take advantage of this, it is your right and yes, it is the greatest arc in your journey which leads to fulfilling your individual goals as well as planetary goals. I will not tell you what it is you need to work on, that should be self-evident to you at this time, after all you have had many moments to figure this out. I will guide you and I will counsel you, however it is you who must do the work. The wheat and chaff have been separated, the veils have been lifted for all to see clearly and the lion is preparing to lay down with the lamb. The emphasis of the masculine and feminine roles are lessoning due in great part to all of you who have united the two sides of yourselves together as one. You are one and yet you are many. Your androgyny is to be held in your highest regards. In due time, none of you should feel inadequate or lacking or in need. You are each Spiritual warriors spearheading the greatest, most monumental changes ever before witnessed on this world. Even in times past when humanity was blessed with the presence of enlightened Beings from all galaxies from all Universes, there was never a moment like this one which is descending upon you now.

OK, take a journey with Me now and listen to My words. How many of you can hear the Song, the everlasting Song of God? It is flowing in the breeze lovingly touching all your senses. Can you hear it? Can you feel My soothing touch upon your brows? There is a silence in the air; a different type of calmness is beginning to prevail through the airways. The silent scream is lessoning, your minds are quieting. You are becoming focused, you are sensing new beginnings, you are feeling a sense of peace sweeping over you from time to time. In TIME it will be permanent. It is now, in this moment, where you can just BE. No cares, no concerns, in the stillness of your minds, you do not feel any draw to become involved in other people's irrational dramas. They are fading away. This stillness, this calmness, is an energy which you can carry with you everywhere you go, whether it is daytime or nighttime. You are home, at least a part of you is, it is that part of you which needs the serenity, the loving feeling one can only find when truly at peace with oneself. Can you feel it? Now take it with you into the dawn's early light, bask in the beauty of the Sun's early glow, and allow it to sooth the yearning for a better time in a better place. You are home and you are on Earth, you **can** be in two places at one time. You exist in the NOW, there is nothing more and nothing less. You are perfect in this moment for you have found perfection, can you feel it? The world around you is in turmoil, hearts and minds are being cluttered with disease and unrest. They can not find the peace they yearn for. They do not know the peace comes from within. They are caught up in the illusions of time. Distance yourself from them, feel your bond with The Creator and the Creation. Absorb the rays which are shining upon you. The world around you may feel upside down, out of focus and dim compared to your Light, you do not need to be a part of it. Can you feel Earth's heartbeat? She draws you near, she is telling you everything is going to be all right, you have nothing to fear. You are living in the NOW, you _are_ the NOW. You are ONE. Carry this feeling with you wherever you go, you are the champions of this Universe, your tales are being told by you. You are revealing to all of Us all that you see, all that you feel, all that you cherish and hold dear. You are Our eyes and ears, you should hold yourself "in proud-ness."

Do not ever again allow yourself to become tangled up in the pettiness which divides the mind from the Soul. You are wondrous. You are the Light. You are God, therefore you are Me, We are one and the same. Through you at this moment I am walking in human form. Soon I will be there with you and I will be walking in mortal form. We as immortals will shake the dust and the cobwebs from those still slumbering. Are your wounds healing, do you feel refreshed and alive, can you _live in the moment_ and **know** _the moment_ is all there is because it is NOW? Can you be satisfied with your inner knowing and be happy for yourself that your inner knowing never needs to be segregated from you ever again? Getting out of your minds and into your hearts is what will see you through even the most stringent of times. Be aware of your surroundings, be

150

a part of what is pure and true and just. You are giants, you are Heavenly, you are "the one" and you are not alone. Find this sense of peace and then you will find there is nothing you can not accomplish. You bear the mark of Myself, you wear the Mantle of Greatness when you can be at peace, when you can find yourself walking in both worlds simultaneously. You do not need to become ensnared in the density of this world; you can bring the higher energies from the highest dimensions into yourself. You can share this, you can spread this tranquility around, and you can interlace it with your own song, your Song of Life. You have each earned the right to have all that you need. Need and desire are not always the same though. I encourage you to enjoy your rewards now for none will be sought later. You are each special, you are each perfect, who could ask for anything more. When you can live in a state of bliss, when you can find yourself lovingly lost in the moment, is when you will be able to do some of your best work. Use that wonderful imagination you have spent many millennia nurturing. If you can accomplish even a small portion of what I have suggested here you will no longer be hurting, for you will have found purpose in your lives. Be good to yourself; learn to like yourself and to love yourself unconditionally. If the others around you chose not to live a life worth living, they are only hurting themselves and any other who will be pulled into their drama; you do not need to be a part of this.

It is difficult to determine which of the two groupings has most difficulty making sense of their lives. Walk-Ins on one hand have to deal with their surroundings which in many cases are not of their own choosing. Yet cope with them they must in order to move on and begin their life anew. You as Starseeds who are not Walk-Ins have had your entire life to nourish good thoughts and remove broken infrastructures and absurdity from your lives. Those who were not successful have set up barriers for themselves which they must overcome. Every person who

enters life here on Earth has a tendency to set up patterns
for themselves, those patterns which allow them to feel
comfortable, to feel as if there is purpose and meaning to
their lives which in many cases is falsely perceived. From
this moment on I encourage each of you to stop trying so
hard, to stop planning for tomorrow and forgetting to live
today. This includes you Walk-Ins too, you should all know
better by now. There is so much you can accomplish in each
and every moment; you can live lifetimes in each day,
month and year that goes by. You can expand time when it
is pertinent to do so. You can walk in the past, the present
and the future all at the same time. You are time-walkers
yes, you have journeyed far to be where you are. The more
you can distance yourself from the affairs of this world
while still being consciously aware of them and doing what
you came here to do, the closer you will be to becoming one
with yourself as Soul. Your outward appearance is not
important, it is just a disguise. It is what lies **within you**,
what attracts your thoughtful gaze, what invigorates,
stimulates and excites you that matters. If you have been
hurt, forget about it. If you feel disappointed in others then
acknowledge to yourself that this is ok. If you feel someone
has wronged you then deal with it or shake it off, you have
better things to do. You have purpose, you ARE a purpose.
Embrace and satiate yourself with the nectar of life, of
Being life and for having chosen life. Relish your
willingness to explore the vast limitless options which
await you. Do so because you can, for so many others who
still slumber in their awakened hours still have no idea of
the true importance of life and the preciousness of this
GIFT.

Now I need to address a subject which I know is near
and dear to so many of My Children at this time. This is a
subject which has caused many a good Soul to fall prey to
its magnetic lure. Part of your missions is to come into
awareness of all that has transpired here in order for you
to make more informed decisions when you are clarifying

information for others. Many still want to know about why things are the way they are on this world and how they came into being. This search, this magnetic draw often is fueled and then fed by those who are in need to dig deeper into certain illusions as they search for the truth. I want you to understand that there are many things which you will not be able to prove in this lifetime to yourself or to others. You will find you can speculate and draw logical conclusions, however you will not know in entirety what it is that began an event or occurrence. Conspiracy theorists of this world unite in their desires to unveil the truth, tragically so many become ensnared in the conspiracies and forget they too have a need to evolve. Evolution does not occur when someone, anyone, is fixated on only certain subject matters which occur in the practical world. It can drain their energy and consume all their waking hours. By all means, explore the conspiracies if you feel you MUST, but do NOT become trapped there. The search for conspiracies and the understanding of these are **NOT** an important stepping stone necessary for each of you to attain higher levels of awareness. Those who become fixated and pour all their energy and time into understanding a conspiracy, any conspiracy, will find the only outcome will be that they will be consumed with anger, hate and distrust. They will no longer be able to see what is right in front of them, for they are continuously straining themselves to find out, "what's wrong with this picture," instead of seeing and knowing when "something is right." Far too many conspiracy theorists' endless relentlessness searching is ruining their minds and that concerns Me. It separates minds from Soul. My hope, Our hope, is that soon each who has pursued this path on a quest for enlightenment will in the very near future be satisfied and simply acknowledge to themselves that some of these devilish things have indeed occurred. These Planetizens need to learn and learn QUICKLY that the knowing and the acknowledgement of all which has been allowed to occur is _THE PAST_ and it is time to let go and live for today. Otherwise Children, it is an endless circle they will find themselves trapped in.

In order to move to a higher level of Soul maturity and Soul knowledge, each of you must complete the cycles you are in, and do so for your own satisfaction as well as for the satisfaction of all who are involved. Life and personal evolution are all cycles which must be undertaken and experienced and for some of you they can seem to happen quickly. They do so because you are able to see, then you understand and then you move on to another cycle because certain lessons no longer fascinate you. What damages the psyche in many Walk-Ins and Starseeds alike is to venture into the Earth Star Realm and have their Spiritual Selves begin to clash with the illusions which appears to be reality. Reality is what you make of it. There are no smoke and mirrors if you maintain your Spiritual equilibrium. If humanity as a whole would have chosen by their own free expression to not fall into the dictums and deceitfulness of others' desires to include many people in their dramas, there would be no dramas to play out. Do you see?

In your quest to honor all those Souls who have been here before you, as well as those who are or will be among the fallen, I suggest that you simply send them your purest thoughts. Praise them all for their willingness to come here during a critical timeline when they are needed the most. Understand their need and their desire to be a part of something greater than themselves. I ask that each of you understand and show great compassion for all especially for those who have fallen, because not everyone was up to the challenge. There is no shame in this, it is what it is. There will be plenty of opportunities for them in their upcoming futures to learn from their errors in judgment. These Planetizens may have recently left Earth wounded by their encounters here, with their Spirits damaged, however they did try. By "trying" I mean they came to

Earth which has never been easy for anyone who has ever incarnated here and tried to make things work out by attempting to make sense out of a denser realm. There is no shame in failing; many apparent failures are actually successes in disguise. Just as many accomplishments which were viewed as successes can actually be considered failures which were set up in order to learn the intended lessons. Yes, I know, it can be complicated. Just do the best you can and in the end just know that it will be all right.

I would encourage each of you take a moment when you feel rested and send your love through the energy of the Christed Light to all those who have **mistakenly** been entrusted to the institutions known as insane asylums and psychiatric wards. Many of these Souls who are in there truly have no grasp on what reality is and will not in this lifetime regain it. However, sadly there are those who entered here with their sentience intact who were intentionally or misguidedly locked away for their own protection. Many of these Planetizens' only crime was that they were feared by other people who were not on the same level of evolvement as they were. The Light you share will help to ease their pain and smooth their transition to Nirvana when their timeline arrives. I am sad to say that many are your Walk-In and Starseed brothers and sisters. And no, I do not want to ever hear any of you say "there but for the grace of God go I." We have already talked about this and there is no need at this time to revisit it. You either remember or you do not. It is for this reason I have encouraged each of you to reread My previous books.

I want you to think about "what if." What if you did not have any more practical world concerns? What if you no longer had any monetary concerns, what if you had all that you really needed? What if no one felt the need to seek and fulfill material desires? What if the world no longer depended upon fossil fuels and the air was miraculously clean and clear? What if the waters once again began to run pure and the lands once again became fertile? What if the children could be children with no hasty or rash desires to grow up too quickly? What if grownups could retain their childhood innocence and live richer, fuller, more stimulating lives because of this? What would you do, what changes would you make in your lives? How do you imagine this would impact upon humanity as a whole? I ask that each of think about this carefully. I will give you a clue, what you think, what you imagine, what you dream of and desire will be the future you are helping to Create. And please do not be concerned about all those Souls who are just beginning to explore the various realms and dimensions and all that these realms offer in lessons. There are many worlds where they can incarnate which will offer them limitless possibilities for Soul growth. You who live the life of the undaunted are the catalysts for this to come into materialization. You do so while filling pages and pages in your "Books of Life."

Whenever you feel doubt or uncertainty about what lies ahead of you please know I will be there with you each step of your journey. Life is about the journey which leads to the destination, so it would be wise of you to be an observer as well as a mover and shaker and live life in the NOW. In this manner you will know that you are moving towards your destination. Although many of you at times feel belittled or abused and some of you have become jaded by living your truths, there is not a single one of you whom I can not say that I am not proud of. Your desire to utilize your freedom of expression is revered and honored. Your choice to live outside the preconditioned norm is much needed at this time. Lack of free expression causes many a goodhearted Soul to sink further into the quicksand of illusion. Be sad for them. BE happy for those who have chosen to rise above the madness like the *phoenix rising from the ashes*. Your woes here are simple and they have expiration dates. Other people here are not so fortunate, not because they are not as evolved as you are; it is because they choose not to rock the boat and chance falling into unknown waters they believe to be uncharted. Columbus was not the first one to find America and Celestial and David and others like them were not the first ones to say, "There is a better way," rather than "there must be a better way." If for but one moment you could believe in yourselves as I believe in YOU, if all of humanity would for just one moment feel this too, then... this would be a hallmark moment. Live well, journey well and know that you will be healed and have your heart's desires.

In loving service to all Wounded Warriors, I dedicate this catalyst to all those who have given so much. *God*

Catalyst 9

White Rose

God ... I want you each to understand that it is always during the beginning of foreseen turbulence on this planet that specific entrances are Created by the Universe HerSelf. This allows major cosmic doorways, sometimes referred to as "channels" to open. There is a specified period of spatialness which We carefully calculate regarding how long these channels will remain open. Once a correct determination of the periods necessary for the openings has been agreed upon, those Beings or those events that must enter are geometrically assigned partners to accompany each of them. In this manner these partners accompanying them assist the Beings or events by bolstering their energies. All those who will enter have prepared for the periodic "journeys by channels" by studiously rehearsing "the where, the why and the how," in order to complete their assigned missions. OK, there are events that require specific types of energies; these energies must be conducive to the task at hand and the upcoming tasks which the initial undertaking will ultimately birth. Although when the channels open whether it is to allow the emergence of Beings or to herald in a certain event, many times the event and the Beings MAY be one and the same. It is difficult to actually separate the Beings from an event anyway. In truth one is but an aspect of the other. You see?

There has never been a period that the Beings who enter through these channels have not been part of an event whether it is a minor or major one. I simply wanted to explain this to you. Personally though, I consider the open channels to be a major event in themselves! When these channels open it is not uncommon to hear some type of sonic noise reverberating in the skies. At times the sky itself may appear to alter its coloration a bit. It does not last long but it lasts just long enough for those timely entrances to take place. Long ago I did tell you all that We have contingency plans always in motion, these plans and their conductors are simply awaiting the call to duty. The channels are always well-guarded by Our Star Keeper Children while the channels are open. When the channels close they do so slowly so it does not cause any atmospheric disturbances. Once the channels are closed they are still well-protected just in case there must for one reason or another need to be a hasty reopening. The reasons for an unscheduled but never unexpected reopening vary. Most of the times these occurrences take place are because more Beings are needed on Earth to bear witness to certain happenings which require clearer vision than the Beings who have already arrived may still have. Although all the Beings who arrive through the channels have remarkably clear vision, there is always a small percentage of them that are affected by the doldrums of the lower energy fields. This can easily interfere with their vision.

All right Planetizens, now that I have given you a basic guided tour of the channels and the reasons for their being needed here, I will continue on with the Beings and events taking place now and in the future, future. I will also reference to the past when I deem it necessary. I do believe that I have given you relevant information in the past, but especially in this particular book about the fact that of necessity there must always be diverse groups of Beings in the higher realms. You know a bit about the Angelic realm for instance. You realize that there are different parts of the Angelic Hierarchy inhabited by Angels of different "ranks." I have in all these books patiently explained about the various Soul levels, Soul stages of maturity and the measurement of Soul growth which all determine the "rank" each Soul has at any given moment. The designated missions which I select for many Souls are of course predicated on all those ranks, karma, determination and strength of a Soul. So it is that with the entrance of a League of eclectic Beings and their partners, they too have been chosen because of their attributes. It does not matter whether I chose them MySelf or they chose themselves with the assistance of their Guides and Master Teachers, for select missions. During a long ago period of the Creation Processing, The Creator decided that there needed to be some other extraordinary Beings to perform extraordinary tasks. But these Beings would remain in the higher realms until He would issue the call. So a new life species was birthed. The Creator sought a certain type of purity, a certain type of innocence and a sweetness and gentleness that could win great victories, but the Beings would also have to share a "Warrior of Spirit" energy as well when called upon to do so.

Granted this is a great deal to expect from Souls. What caused it to become an alliance of Spirit was the fact that The Creator insisted that these Souls would only descend into the madness that was already birthed on the Earth Star planet at certain time periods when their assistance was most needed here. They would have to simply follow through with their tasks and then depart. However, each person who would ever incarnate here who shared a symbiotic and sympathetic energy with these other Life Forms, would weave the shared energy from this League into the very core of their own Souls and carry it within themselves throughout their mortal lives here. Other than the time periods when they needed to descend, this League was to remain in the higher realms and teach others there. No Children, their life missions were different from your own. The other Luminescents and I met with The Creator and We all suggested that a specific energetic name signature be given to them. Spontaneously We all had the same telepathic thought of the same name signature. They would always and forever be known as, "White Rose." As members of White Rose they do and always will exhibit a purity of Spirit in such manner that you could almost say they seem to always remain apart from humankind in one sense, yet are among the staunchest Beings ever Created. They love humanity dearly. Although individually they do of course possess their own names, the themes of the names are always of a Celestial nature. As a collective We simply call them White Rose. Each of them is well-aware of which of them We speak with individually, they do not have any need to use their personal names for that.

White Rose is androgynous of course, yet always selects a gender to portray here on this planet in order to better serve humanity, but above all to serve the Universe to the best of their abilities. For to serve humanity IS to serve the Universe and they know this well. Because of the purity and special sense of peace they carry with them they are often confused with Angels while they are incarnate here. For the last 10 years and three months they have been arriving here in **massive** numbers and had begun working with some of the youngest children, but especially with autistic people of all age groups. Millions and millions and millions of My Children here have been touched by White Rose again and again and again. Some of the White Rose Beings have been assigned to work with certain individuals who have "fallen." Their White Rose coalition needs little help from humanity though. They tend to migrate to other locations every few months or every couple of years, although some of them have been called upon to linger longer in some places than are others. Their presence can actually startle some people, these are the fallen ones who refuse to leave the illusions behind, they are startled enough that they awaken. This happens because White Rose is an absolutely powerful League that does not indulge in power plays. They simply ARE power and peace and they wear the Badge of Honor. OK, all of you Advocates have interacted with White Rose "for as long as you have been." Although you knew that when the greatest periods of inhumanity would occur that would be when White Rose would arrive, there is still not too high of a percentage of you who are aware of the changes in the continuum when the League enters here. The nanosecond of their arrivals touches lifeforms all over this world. The White Rose collective immediately sends themselves out to whatever person or location is part of their assigned mission. If you can imagine a tree with huge limbs that appears to always be in an expansive position simply because the limbs are part of something well-rooted in its own foundation, that may help to give you a better idea of what White Rose is. They are not simply individuals, they are also part of something greater than themselves, yet without the White Rose the greater could be less. Do you understand?

White Rose activates specific triggers that were designed with YOU in mind. For some of you the triggers exist as physicals changes; anomalies such as suddenly finding a small mark on your body that you do not remember having before. For some Planetizens it is a sudden special feeling that someone is gently touching the hair on their heads, or the hair on their arms etc. Others of your groupings will suddenly feel a state of inner peace, for White Rose lifts you to a different level known as, "a state of grace." And of course all Advocates' Souls begin a wonderful swirling motion as they themselves receive vast amounts of high Spiritual energy. White Rose members are expert warriors as I mentioned before; but it is because they must be and they CAN be. They can suddenly appear on battlefields just long enough to save lives, but are seldom identified as anyone in particular. Now one of the triggers they set into activated motion is a trigger of "self-release." This measuring movement is necessary in order to determine whatever amount of density existing in Souls, especially Advocates' Souls, has taken on fear issues. This then is when White Rose works intensely with the personality as well as with the individual Soul. Advocates who have been subjected to psyche attack though are the first ones they seek to aid. As they do so the personality may be able to come to terms with itself and understand WHY there is fear present, when it KNOWS there should not be. Then Soul Voice speaks with personality and at the very least a truce can be issued while the personality tries to quell its reactions to unfounded fears. Soul and White Rose know the perceptions of the fears implanted through psyche attack are but illusions. And furthermore, NOW because of these long-lasting periods of inner turbulence and civil unrest all over this planet, the spatial periods of the continuation of the incoming of White Rose energies are at a crucial juxtaposition. Psyche attacks when existing in massive numbers CAN cause disturbances in the continuum. Did you know that? Even though the continuum does actually have its own orbit and its own grid which interlocks with all Universes, a disturbance caused by dark matter CAN impact on the further expansion of the continuum at any given moment.

The interaction between each of you and White Rose is an incredible example of what your love, great devotion and impeccable integrity can accomplish TOGETHER today, just as it had when White Rose individually and collectively had integrated with all of you long, long ago. When this initially occurred, you were given small strands of White Rose energy which you lovingly and eagerly accepted. You have all learned what indelible fingerprints are; well the White Rose strands which are finely matched energy streamers are also an integral part of your off-world identification of self, which will always be with you. White Rose's mission includes sending minute imagings and thoughts to you during specific spatial periods which are the defining moments of when you need White Rose memories and energies the most. There is great humor here Children; I have watched you respond to White Rose throughout each life experience you have had to date. Yet in some of those lifetimes many of you were unknowing of what White Rose beauty truly held for you. Oftentimes I have heard many of you remark that you prefer different colored roses. That is fine too, just please remember it is White Rose who beckoned to you to remember your origins which are conjoined with White Rose's own.

OK now, because of the wondrous Advocacy Agreement you are part of, certain stages of memory recall had been given to you in each lifetime but particularly in this one, regarding White Rose. White Rose calls upon you each to savor the inner peace and joy they send to you. To experience the ultimate "highs" of love is to experience White Rose. To feel the greatest of compassion for all others whether you know them or not, is to be more completely aligned with White Rose. To try to define the exact sensations an Advocate experiences when thinking of White Rose is difficult; the sensations vary with each individual of course, but as a collective you are strengthened impressively by the energies of White Rose. White Rose strengthens the Resonance Cord you have; that alone should cause you to better understand the power and strength White Rose possesses. I have asked My Celest-Self if she would agree to share one of her many, many experiences with White Rose that she has had in this lifetime. She agreed to do so, so I am going to ask her to write about it now.

Celest - each and every time I have encountered White Rose energies, wonderful gifts are sent to me. Gifts that Create life-lasting memories; ones that I am constantly revisiting whenever I feel the need to, or when White Rose suggests that I do so. A particular one that I keep revisiting though, especially in the last couple of weeks, is the only one I will speak about. When I was living on the east coast I awakened one night, actually it was 3 a.m. with absolutely no idea at all about what had caused me to awaken then. I decided to go into my living room and sit on the couch for a few minutes and see if I could find out what was going on. The moon was high in the sky and was shining a great deal of moonlight into the room, I really

164

enjoyed that! There I was sitting on the couch; I looked across from myself at the television set that was of course turned off. Within perhaps two seconds of looking at the blank screen, all of a sudden the Crystal City appeared on the screen, on the <u>turned off</u> set. I sat there laughing with great delight and thanking Tomás and all the other elders there for sharing the City with me. Although I go to the Crystal City whenever I want to, it was the first time that the City came to me. I was so happy, but it was not an "Earth-born happiness." It was an incredibly elevated state of the feeling of "being home" that I felt. Then within seconds while I was watching the goings-on in the City, I suddenly felt a satiny and silky feeling of something touching the backs of my hands. I looked at my hands and was astonished to see that White Roses were covering first my hands, then my head and then my entire body. I looked around at the entire room and saw hundreds and hundreds of White Roses cascading from above into the room and touching everything. They all came through the ceiling and as they touched everything, they would suddenly disappear into whatever they were landing on. On the floor they simply passed through the floor. This went on for quite a while and as all this was happening, the City on the blank screen began to glow and undulate in a beautiful movement. Eventually the roses stopped falling into the room and the City disappeared from view. I felt the most wondrous state of empowerment, of the greatest off-world love and I felt total peace. I re-experienced the total emancipation that I have when I am back on my home world. I can return to this memory again and again and re-experience ALL THAT IS and ever shall be. This is all I want to say about this event, God.

God ... Thank you Celestial; I do completely understand how you are feeling about this. It is a normal reaction to *The Greatest Story Ever Told of the Greatest Love Ever Had*. OK now, White Rose is always in touch with each of you regardless of whether you have issued the call for her

165

to do so or not. It is what she does. Those Planetizens among all the groupings here who have asked to be in conscious alignment with White Rose are forever encountering various objects that White Rose sends to them. It may be clothes, statues, books and so forth, that all bear the picture or an image of White Rose. A few of you more fortunate ones will at times see a picture of White Rose with a few white doves encircling her. White Rose is truly an Omnipresent part of the Advocacy Agreement. I made mention of the fact that White Rose always enters with geometrically chosen partners. This is part of the Creator's agreement with White Rose. The partners must always be on the same levels as the ones they are accompanying, in this manner they "speak the same language," yet are adept at using Sacred Geometry as a means of assisting all Planetizens here. The partners are from many diverse realms. Some are Angels; others are discarnate Spirit Beings who have not spent any lifetimes on the Earth Star planet. Yet each chosen partner must agree to assist White Rose and must be fully capable of connecting with each of the groupings here, whether they know the individuals or not. The partners are an all-inclusive force of ethereal Beings in one sense, yet they do carry with them the knowledge which they have garnered from the Crystal City. No, it is not unusual for discarnate Beings who have never spent any lifetimes here on this planet to be sent here or ask to be sent here in order to be of assistance. They have chosen never to live here, understandably, but that in no way deters them from helping humankind. So it is that White Rose and company work together with an absolutely flawless, awesome, combination of energies in order to successfully fulfill their missions. White Rose and the partners are collectively in a continuous state of transmitting information to the higher realms. This assists all of Us in further determining how much longer White Rose must continue to envelop this world. This is very crucial information. Crucial to Us and especially most crucial to all of **you!** I am now asking each of you to become more adept in determining when White Rose is among you. Pay more attention to when White Rose signals to you, at times it may be through the scent of the White Rose. I am also asking each of you to learn to call White Rose to you, if you have not already. It is merely a matter of thinking "White Rose," surely you can make time to do that, can you not? Each person White Rose touches in whatever manner Rose chooses will go on to touch others with White Rose energies. It is the Advocacy's manner of expanding upon the bridge which each Advocate assisted in erecting long, long ago. This is the bridge you must each cross over now, it is the bridge which leads you all safely to eternity. *White Rose HOLDS the bridge in her loving hands; she will never let you fall!*

Over the next few years a new type of movement will begin here. We will actually try to implement this movement in mid-summer of 2015. This will be White Rose working with a select group of Advocates here and assisting them with simply working with Terra, while some other Advocates and White Rose will be working with non-mammal life forms. The Devic kingdom has requested to be permitted to work with these Advocates and White Rose as well, and I assure you that request will also be honored! White Rose may enter here through a few different avenues. Many of them enter during the birthing time of a new child. They, along with the child's natural bevy of Guardian Angels, share the responsibility of looking out for the vested interests of the newborn babe for an allotted period of time. The Angels remain, but White Rose then goes on to work with older children, especially those who are in great danger of falling, particularly those children whose parents and other family members had fallen. White Rose is only able to work with small numbers of Earth Seeds, for reasons which should be obvious to you all. Star Seeds and especially Walk-Ins are ALWAYS in the company of White Rose, whether they know it or not. At times White Rose accompanies the Walk-Ins as they are entering into a human body.

Then again White Rose always works with the flora and fauna here and provides nourishment for them because their natural protection from pollutants has been weakened. White Rose and partners may simply choose to "zoom in" and just suddenly materialize here. How they arrive is their choice; but it is always under the auspices of Universal Laws. At times they choose to wear human guises and do so very well. Yet their very presences Create a beautiful vortex of energy and peacefulness wherever they go. You will soon see a couple of them, how many more choose to "go public," is up to them.

From this moment on, many of you who are reading this will begin to awaken even more so than you have already. Your clarity and intuitiveness will begin to astound you. You see, you are reaching a pivotal juxtaposition in your lives; it is one you have been waiting for even though you did not know what it was you were anticipating. The infusions of Light matter into this world are being accelerated in minute degrees at every moment now. And you are the catalyst for this. As more and more of My Children begin to awaken from their slumbers they will be acting in a sense like lightning rods. They will be magnetizing themselves to the energy streamers being sent here from all Universes and all of Creation. We, with the assistance of all the advanced races of Beings from all of the higher realms are continuously as a collective sending Our genetic encoding to each of you. Although We have been doing this, now We need to accelerate the process. In this manner We will be effectively stimulating the dormant parts of minds and hearts, thus freeing your Spirits to soar to new and more refined heights. Do not be surprised if one moment you are crying and you do not know why, while simultaneously you find yourself smiling. You may compare this experience to seeing a newborn child entering into this world, or receiving your first kiss from your first true love. As I have mentioned in the past the Universe is free-flowing, she stimulates all the centers of the matrixes of all Souls. She does so while entrusting them to continue to expand upon the elation of Be-ing, of flying unfettered while still Earthbound.

OK, as White Rose and all the other accompanying Beings who enter this realm touch you through the magnificence of their auras and their endlessly beautiful energy fields, you will begin to feel lighter, less tethered to the material world and more at ease with yourself. The reason this is occurring is because you are finally beginning to feel a sense of peace within yourself, this is what you can only find when you are at home among those who you are closest to, or NOW experiencing because of the dedication of these Beings who are among you. You are being brought the essence of your home worlds and these essences are infusing those energies into your own personal worlds and your immediate surroundings. Each object you touch will gather great luminescence from your gentle embrace. The people around you will begin to feel a sense of amusement, amusement in the sense that they too will begin to feel lighter and less burdened by their perception of the blandness of their lives. No, I am not saying everyone's lives are bland; for indeed they are not. However, even the most free-Spirited person can feel the immenseness of the energies of pure love being subtly intertwined with their own energies, thus providing a needed boost for them. The Children of the inner-world are beaming with delight each time this occurs. For them this means that soon they too will be able to rejoin their relations. These are the relations on Earth who they chose to separate themselves from long, long ago. The doors to inner-Earth will in the not to distant future begin to open. As this occurs, the New People of the New Earth will be joined with those who long ago sought shelter from the madness taking place above ground. Great teachers will walk among you; this world will expand and grow infinitely more beautiful. The Master Teachers who are among you now as well as *The Masters led by Master Kato,* will guide you and comfort you when the need arises to do so. They will do so with the assistance of White Rose.

If you have not yet done so, now would be a good time to call upon your individual Master Teachers to embrace you. Call upon The Masters of all races to Light the way for you. Call upon The Masters and Master Kato as well. You can work in tandem with White Rose and infuse the very matrix of this world with all the love, peace and happiness each of you desires and which your Souls need. *CREATE the THOUGHTS and make it so!* Connect with your Soul Clusters, you do so every day of your life anyway, so why not do so with purpose now? If you have an idea, a proposal you would like to suggest, then call upon the Collective Consciousness of **All That IS** to work with you and more importantly *through you,* to bring your ideas, and your inspirations into manifestation. The OverSoul of the Soul Clusters invites everyone to share new stimulating ideas that will be entered into the endless pools of possibilities. I ask you all to remember that when the Silent Scream can be heard no more is when the state of ultimate peace will be here on this planet. You should each know by now that your realistic desires combined with those desires of others of likemind is when you can accomplish almost anything you set your heart and Soul on achieving. Freedom of choice known by Us as *Freedom of Expression,* is a gift, a very special gift entrusted to all Souls by The Creator HimSelf. Use it <u>wisely</u> and you will never be wrong. Remember, there are certain things you can do that you MUST do. You must respect the Universal Laws of governance and respect others' free expression. Honor the elements and you honor yourself. <u>Issue the call,</u> this is something that I keep repeating throughout this book. Need I mention it again? You are The Second Coming; there will be no need for a third. You are the Christ

Consciousness; this Consciousness knows no bounds or limitations, no restrictions either. PLEASE, do not impose any on yourself. You are White Rose, or eventually you will be. Each time you are touched by these wondrous Souls you become more and more like them. Expect a miracle and you become the miracle, can you understand?

Now as each of you embraces the expansion of yourselves through the intimate process of remembering all that I am sharing with you, I must caution you to stop expecting so much from yourselves. Your evolvement as an individual must occur in steady, measured sequences. The human body and mind are remarkable in their design and they require gentle infusions when amassing more Light particles. There must be balance; otherwise you would be bouncing up and down like a yo-yo out of control. Be patient with your progress, this is not a race where you have to come in first place, for there is no finish line. You will continue to evolve until the day you transition from this world and We will all be waiting for you with open arms. White Rose knows which of you is ready for more infusions because she monitors your Resonance Cord. At no time will White Rose or any of Us attempt to thrust you beyond your limits, that would be counterproductive and completely insensitive to your needs. We all are aware of your desires for instantaneous change to be brought to this world. That My dear ones, is not going to happen, not in the sense you would like to see it happen that is. Until the Collective Consciousness has achieved an undeniable pivotal point for change, while the rest of humanity chooses to alter the course of reality upon this world, We ask that you PLEASE be satisfied with what **IS** shifting for the better.

You can all help Us in this matter by taking personal responsibility for your own self and being respectful of all you are entrusted with. Your roles as the caretakers of this world are equal with the care you take in honoring yourself. If any of Us White Rose included, did not take into consideration your current level of awareness as well as your physical health, then We would be doing you an injustice. A snail may take longer to cross the road than say a rabbit may, however the snail as slow as it is, would observe and absorb so much more detail of its surroundings as it breathes in all that it sees in its progressively patient journey. Humanity is the only impatient life form on this world. The patient observer sends clearer unfiltered information back to those of Us who must cope with the hard decisions to be made concerning who is progressing and who is not. Then the decisions may become written in stone about "who and what" will be able to survive in the higher frequencies Terra is propelling herself towards. In this manner with the information We receive from all of you, We will be able to better determine where White Rose is needed the most. White Rose has an infallible ability to multitask, but even they know when to stop with one person and move on to another. Freedom of expression is always to be honored, even if you are an ancient Soul whose mission is of great importance. Remember I have told you several times that there are always contingency plans which can be initiated in a moment's notice if certain overlying circumstances take place. Starseeds, you are My steady rudder, Walk-Ins, you are the stimulus needed to make sure the waters do not become glossed over with the stagnant pools of complacency. Because of this I want to point out that many Walk-Ins and Starseeds alike have written into their Soul Contracts that if they find themselves unable to achieve what they came here to do, that they will be willing to return home and let another step in and take their place. This is always the greatest intersection when White Rose steps in to lend a helping hand to those in this predicament. White Rose does not cajole, she suggests, lends moral support and offers her guidance. White Rose knows that this situation is like running a race and when a person's time has come, she assists in passing the baton on to the next runner. Be aware that White Rose is assisting you throughout this special type of Olympics.

OK now, it is time to remind you of the importance White Rose plays in interacting with the Star Keeper forces that are always in motion above this planet, as well as those forces that are on this Earthly plane. The Star Keepers themselves are of course in full awareness of the Advocacy Agreement and of the vast importance the roles White Rose must play, as well as what their chosen missions are here in the Earthly Realm. It is with their assistance along with the assistance of White Rose and all of Creation, that Terra's new Galaxy is being further expanded. I told you before that no one can do everything all by themselves without overdoing it and this is a perfect example of that. Many times those Star Keepers, who have aligned with you as a means to assist you in fulfilling your personal as well as planetary missions, call upon White Rose to be the catalyst to buoy the spirits of certain people who can not seem to calm their sense of restlessness. This usually happens when an individual or groups of individuals are under duress. There are times when the Guides or others who aligned with those who have entered the Earth Star Realm are as unable as I am to reach the despondent Soul. Often times a simple "flyby" by those Star Keepers who are from the individuals' home worlds, whether the people are Walk-Ins or Starseeds can cause a sense of excitement, or at times anticipation to blossom in their sub-conscious. This may be just the catalyst needed to stimulate an upward flow of energies to the individuals and to curtail the downward spiral they had been experiencing. When missions such as this happen it is the minute infusions of White Rose energies that prevail. There is no limit to what, where, or when, they may enter to perform miracles, particularly in times when they are needed the most. To each of you Planetizens who respond to White Rose, I salute you.

"Here is a sketch Celest drew of two members of *White Rose* who recently descended here and offered to pose for her. They expressly gave permission for their picture to be part of this book."

I am dedicating this segment to White Rose with My eternal gratitude. *God*

Catalyst 10

The Wonder of You

God ... Well Children, how are you feeling now that you are learning so very much about yourselves? Are your minds still reeling? Have you been able yet to feel as though your feet are touching the ground again? Now for the BIG question ... are you still wondering why I have waited so long to bring your consciousness into My confidence about all of this? OK, here is the situation: I have quietly been in the background of your lives throughout every incarnation you have ever had. When We are all together at home though, that is a different matter. I am not all that quiet when home with each of you, or so I have been told by My Celest-Self, but then neither is she! While I have been accompanying each of you in your journeys here, but especially in this particular one, I have had to await a specific spatial gridline intersection for these books to be written. As far as the timing was concerned, it HAD to be the exact nano-minute which had been decreed by The Creator before even the first words of the first book were permitted to be written. Then, it was crucially important that I only reveal so much information to you in each of the books. This is where it may seem to you to be silly because so many of you Advocates try to assimilate all knowledge you are able to, but try to do so ALL the time.

Although I do indeed applaud your individual and collective enthusiasm, too much information being shared with you could actually have caused you harm. Your desires to share your truths and reveal too much Spiritual knowledge with others would have placed you in some tempestuous situations in the past 20 years. Also there is the fact that as long as you are wearing the guise of mortality, you must remember that the human brain can only handle a certain amount of information, otherwise it could be overloaded and then it would short-circuit. So, this having been said, I will continue with the why and the how. I had many centuries ago already laid out the information I was to reveal to all of you in the necessary increments you could safely handle. This way I could carefully monitor you each and observe you as your understandings became more clear to you. But you still needed to have the necessary time periods for adapting to the "new" knowledge before I was prepared to share another book with you. So, I have not been surprised at all to watch a great number of you actually <u>seem</u> to fall asleep when reading any of these books that have so far been written. Although the sleepers appeared to feel a bit sheepish when they realized they fell asleep while reading, I actually expected this to happen. It was when you **thought** you were sleeping that other events took place. This was when Soul Voice was using great skill and great Creativity by allowing your minds to rest, while Soul itself carefully brought peace to your minds about all that you were learning. This permitted you to awaken and return to reading when you were ready to, but allowed your Super Consciousness to expand itself, thereby RAISING you to a greater level of understanding and enhancing your states of consciousnesses.

Remember I said I have contingency plans? Well, these included allowing you your freedom of reading, BUT slowing you down when it was clearly indicated to Me and to Others that it was necessary to do so. So, while I had been placing all the information in a sequential order that I knew you would all benefit from the most, I did this because I understood the different information that needed to be in each book. I also knew that this book, *Advocates for Justice,* would be *the one* you were ready for NOW and why it had to be so. There was no possible way I could have spoken with any of you about the Advocacy or your roles as Advocates before now. I suppose you could compare this situation to the role a good school teacher has in KNOWING what to teach and when to teach it.

OK, many preset signals that have been placed within your Soul matrixes began to immediately respond to My written words. This was quite intentional on My part and agreed to by you per the Advocacy Agreement. I have and still am experiencing such great delight as I watch you each savor the written words in these books. You do so while you have still been achieving a new "stature" of both your SoulSelves as well as the tangible changes your personalities have been making. So much love! I feel so much love emanating from you each, yet it is also happening collectively. You are lighting up this Universe and many Universes behind her! I truly wish you could see yourselves through My eyes. I wish you could feel My love for you in the same way as I feel your love for Me. I want you one and all to please STOP thinking about mistakes of judgment you may have made in this lifetime. That is the past and this is the present. It is all that you do and say and feel NOW that is a major defining moment of your lives! *This is the time period you have been waiting for.* Equate it with the new YOU that you are rapidly becoming. I ask no more of you than that. Do so for yourselves individually and collectively and for the Jesus THE Christ Consciousness you truly are. You do not walk alone here; you never have. I would never permit that to happen! Do you understand this? Planetizens, a clearly defined event is taking place here; you are now standing in pride and some of you are having mixed emotions. I do understand this so please, male and female alike cry if it will help you to cope with either the new flow of emotions or the new comprehension which accompanies these emotions. Do so because you can and because it is a good thing to do. It is NOT weakness that causes this; it is the releasing of the old and the embracing of the new. You can do no wrong!

I have thoroughly enjoyed and embraced the wonderment I see in your minds. I am in-gratitude to you as I watch you each grounding yourselves in the new and better aligned thought patterns and thought forms you are bringing into your lives. These are priceless gifts you are sharing with yourself. They are incomparable in every way, please never forget that. Throughout the rest of your mortality here you shall be blessed with a special type of honor, it is a commemoration which We dedicate to you. It is about your Soul beauty which will live and thrive throughout eternity with a special proclamation which resonates with the remembrances of all that you are, all that you do and all that you will continue to do.

OK, yes I have heard you wondering about men, women and younger people who have transitioned from this Earthly existence; so many of you are sad believing that those Children did not have the opportunity to be Advocates. You are wrong. Many of them were also Advocates. Yes, those who were also Advocates did indeed accomplish a great many wonderful achievements prior to their journey to Nirvana. They did want to stay longer here, those who still had good physical health; but they had arrived at their own personal mortal intersection and returned home. Well before *their journey* took them to Nirvana though, at the point of their exiting mortality, they had their Guides, Master Teachers and beautiful Angels with them. Those Beings each reassured the departing Souls that they had indeed accomplished more than they had realized while mortal. This is why "THOUGHT," is so critically important to all of you while you are still in mortality. Shortly before one passes over to make their final transition, their own Angels, Guides and Master Teachers send to them countless messages, dreams and imagings which clearly show the good works they had accomplished through thought alone. Sometimes the personality will retain a minute aspect of those passionately whispered messages and imagings.

Sometimes it does not. All then is predicated upon the individual's state of mind, health and the level of their state of grace. I have gone to great lengths in these books to remind you over and over again that you NEVER make that final journey alone. So PLEASE, stop feeling sad when remembering those you love who have traveled on to the Greatest Road. They were brought into a state of awareness of their accomplishments, just as each of you will be when the "time" for your personal mortal intersection arrives and you must travel it. The difference for you here and now is that because you have been learning through these books, you will have a greater impact on others while you are still mortal. Meanwhile, those who have already left are having a greater impact on **you** than you realize! That is indeed part of the pact of *promises made and promises kept.*

I do see in the minds and hearts of some of you who have suffered serious health problems which can not be reversed that you know you are now facing your mortal end. You are the Children I will now address: you have done so much for so many people and yet some of them have not always reciprocated. Oftentimes you have felt so alone, so misunderstood because of your beliefs and yet you had the courage to carry on and do what you could while learning all that you were able to. Your good deeds and your impeccable desires to simply do what you have been able to, even if you have not been aware of what you were doing, have **never** gone unnoticed by any of Us. You share the same badge of honor as do those others here whose mortality timelines have not arrived yet. We are sending some special Envoys to you who will also be accompanying you during the journey home. You will be able to feel their presences, if you want to that is. Their presences are the warmth, the circling Light beams and the soft gentle sounds you will hear. They cherish you as do I. You have earned your rewards. Your ending is merely your new beginning. *Journey well.*

OK, it is with great joy that I have been recently able to see many of the younger people here finally becoming disgusted with the injustice people have been subjected to, to such a degree that they are now "investigating" the Spiritual side of life here and comparing it to what they thought life was about. You will be in contact with some of these Planetizens, many of you already know some of them or have heard about them. When it is time for these other younger Planetizens to seek your advice, please share your words and truths with them. Do not talk over their heads though, remember that they are still in the "struggling to understand state" that so many of you have already experienced, or are experiencing now. Please speak of what you know and say, "I don't know," when the questions they ask you are ones you do not have the answers to just yet. I can not call them "Advocates in-training," for that would be untrue. All Advocates who enter this world do so with the Advocacy Agreement seated within their Souls, just waiting for the intersection to unveil itself when they too will enter into a state of realization of their shared missions here. Just because a person may be young chronologically does not mean that they are young Spiritually. The same is true in reverse. An older person may be older chronologically, but much younger Spiritually. I ask that you each remember this fact. It is always quite simple to be able to tell the difference when the issue is the "age" of the Spiritual person and the "age" of one who is not yet awakened. I also want you to better understand that sometimes those who have been sleeping do awaken with a strange desire to make up for lost time. I personally know many of you Planetizens who have done this yourselves. Do not assume anything based on age. Many of today's younger Children who are being blessed through the touch of White Rose will develop into some of the greatest Advocates this world has ever seen. Also, White Rose is working diligently with the Star Light

Children and those Children will also begin working with the younger Advocates.

Now that I have mentioned this to you there is still a bit more I need to share. I would very much appreciate it if each of you can make time when you are able to and think back to when you began reading these books. Try to remember if you can not only how much you learned, but also think back to what the books have accomplished for you. I will give you some reminders of what I have seen and heard from you individually and collectively. I have been blessed with enjoying the wonder of you as you arrived at so many greater understandings. These understandings have been about so many experiences you have had, both the good and the not so good, about thoughts you have had, companions you have been with and yet learning in a better way why you are here. I too have benefitted greatly by your actions and reaction to My words. My Omnipresent love for you each has swelled to such a degree that even The Creator noticed the changes to My own image. The love I share with you and you share with Me are the greatest of any gifts I could ever receive! As for each of you, I have been honored by your presence as you began to make significant progress and yet you <u>still</u> are achieving on a higher level the more elevated states of personal evolution, while affecting planetary and interplanetary evolution in the greatest manner ever conceived.

I actually was laughing with pure joy as so many of you altered your strides and began to strut with inner pride as you arrived at the true realization of who you are and how you "came to be." To observe the glistening tears of joy, to feel your sense of vindication and to feel your innate understanding suddenly change is just precious. Your understanding suddenly achieved a new hue as We watched your Souls glowing with explicable happiness. For Me and all of Us who are the Luminescents, I must tell

181

that it gives Us all great pleasure in knowing that you are entering into the prime of your lives. And, you are doing so, *the right way!* It is rare that We see this in Planetizens here, but the changes you are Creating are undeniable, and unmistakable. As you finished one book after another yes even you Children who read the books out of order, the fog of unknowingness began to lift from your inner countenance. What is equally important for you to know though is that if you read each book countless times, you will be pleasantly surprised by a few things that will happen. These things are important for you to know about. Each book raises you to higher state of consciousness; as this occurs what you have reread begins to feel strangely normal and ordinary. BUT, then you will find that there is more information that you are reading about that you have no memory of having read in the books before. That too was preplanned for you. You see My Children, once your consciousness has been elevated your Super Consciousness and the Magna Consciousness enter and subtly for the most part, you begin to see other words, knowledge and wisdom that have been encapsulated within each page. It is then that these Consciousnesses reveal additional information for you. Each of these books have been painstakingly written without editing in order for all these "trigger memories" to surface for you.

OK, I will only tell you now that because of all that you are learning, all that you are truly either understanding or beginning to understand, you are unconsciously affecting all the great changes this planet is in such need of. Now, that having been said, I ask you each to seriously contemplate how much greater the changes will be when you focus CONSCIOUSLY and use thought to Create miracles. We all know you can do this, because it is what *you as Advocates do!*

The mirrors in your minds' eyes are rapidly beginning to reflect back to you all that We see. You are becoming ever

182

more aware of the perils humanity as a whole faces in the times ahead, as they too try to make sense of all that is ongoing here. They are trying to understand this by using logic and reason when their focus should be trying to understand why any of this level of insanity ever came to be in the first place. This is another reason why you as the Advocates are here. It is not by any stretch of the imagination the only reason of course; however it is a very important one. I feel compelled to tell you again that I want you to know not only how proud I am of each of you; I want you to also know that this lifetime in particular is all about you. You have been chosen for your strengths as well as for your weaknesses. Weaknesses are overcome by working through them, and perceived weaknesses may be nothing more than self-reflections. These reflections may merely be ones which <u>you</u> may be misinterpreting. These misrepresentations by you could be that you see yourselves as not being good enough or not having enough to teach others. This is a two-fold fear: it also includes that you may feel you are not living up to your full potential. None of you are perfect; yet conversely you **are** perfect in every moment. It is your individual differences in the ways you project yourselves as outward movements of your inner momentum and the various ways that you each speak, which separate you from the others who like you, are still in the process of trying to understand it all. Mannerisms, attitude, and respect for oneself are defining attributes each of you possesses which are your own individual Mantles of Greatness. You have no need to wear a sash across your chest that defines your merit badges to show your accomplishments and credits to your character and poise. This would be superficial and it is superficiality that has consumed many a good-natured Soul. Everyone has their own way of just trying to figure it all out, and that is not always as easy to do as it may seem it should be.

You are entering into a new phase of humanity, one where kindness and love and an overall concern for all of humanity will come into the forefront of life. It will be one of your highest priorities. A reality you should <u>always</u> remember is that each and every Earth Star walker from the earliest beginnings of this planet, needed to learn firsthand how to deal with the darkness in order for them to appreciate the Light. The challenges were many then and now, but the rewards for overcoming the challenges without compromising yourselves, are incomparable. Throughout the rest of your mortality you should continue to be proud of yourself. I hasten to caution you though not to prejudge anyone who is still here now, or anyone who has recently departed from this world. You do not at this time have sufficient knowledge of the others' life lessons to know if they succeeded or not during this lifetime. As I have implied before, many times failing or losing at something is really succeeding and winning. Can you understand this? It is very important that you do. Please continue to steer your course through life skillfully, be the ultimate observers, continue to bear witness and do not be hasty to judge those who are just now awakening. Remember the different hats people wear and their varied purposes for doing so. Your warrior Spirits thrive on a challenge, but I implore you one and all just do not "overdo" the challenges! Your healing and loving Spirits cause you at times to try to "fix" others, this is not wise. You guide them best when you are teaching by example; leave the "fixing" to Us, or leave it to the ones who need to "fix" themselves.

OK, before you start celebrating "the great changeover," let Me remind you that when I speak of "time," in many instances it seems to you to take longer than you may like. Although I do believe that it will still require what could be considered as some linear time for all the changes in this world to occur, expansiveness must take place in the hearts and minds of all who still have their generational curses to work through. Many of these Planetizens are being confronted with the patterns of lifetimes of mistakes and they still need to remove those patterns from their lives. There is still much left to do. Maintain your forward momentum and continue to look for the signs of change, and then read the signs correctly. Remain in the flow of the winds of change and you will be where you need to be when the time is right.

No matter how many times I see one of you coming to the "ah ha," moment when you realize something that has been blocking you for so long becomes apparently clear to you, I have heard so many of you say, "I should have known better, or I should have known that." I am personally pleased when the realizations become clear to you as you realize you now understand the situations. These realizations at times come rushing in as torrents of waves of understandings. At times the floodgates you protectively installed in your intellects come crashing down then and that is a good thing. The retraining of your minds to allow them to function as they were always intended to, instead of the protective guardians they became as you fought your way through every moment of your life, can be quite debilitating. Learning to understand the Spiritualness of all things both great and small is not always an easy concept to grasp. But you have been achieving this.

As your Light shines further into the darkness and continues in its loving way of challenging people to look deeply into their own selves, all too often selfish, petty, arrogant people will continue to do what they do. This is of no concern to you any longer. You must work with the ones who earnestly seek your guidance; this can only be found with the fellowship that occurs among truly goodhearted, likeminded individuals. We have spent considerable time discussing amongst Ourselves as well as with individual Souls and their Soul Clusters, the best way to proceed with the selfish, petty, arrogant people from this point on. So, the decision has been made to treat them in accordance with what they have done or said and its relativity to the

185

ways they have treated others. We formatted a bit of a different plan for them. They will be lovingly received when they transition from this world and after a **lengthy** period of self-examination, We will assist them in seeking lifetimes in locations which are best suited for their individual Soul's growth. No one is being penalized here. Consider it to be more of a slap on the wrist they will each be receiving for not paying attention when those who love them the most beckoned to them to sit down and listen.

The shy and timid Planetizens among you are in <u>many</u> cases among the most humble and respectful Children here and have a deep Soul appreciation for all which they are blessed with. My greatest request of each of you in this moment is that you continue to strive to impress upon yourselves the importance of being "you," BUT <u>for</u> you, <u>not</u> for anyone else. You are each blossoming into such fine expressions of yourselves that although I notice it, you do not always see what I see. You are the jewels of the Universes; you are no longer diamonds in the rough. You who are My emissaries, please carry yourself with pride, present yourself with dignity, and never demean yourself by being arrogant or vain. You are on a higher level of evolvement than many others are, yet at one time you did indeed walk in their shoes. Go forth and spread good will and honorable intent. If you are sitting in peace and enjoying the present moment, then you are doing exactly what you should be right now. If you are sharing your truths with those who will listen, then in this moment you are doing what you should be. If you are studiously rereading My words as a means to better understand what I am sharing with you, then you are doing exactly what you should be in this moment. These types of moments are important. In others words, relax and remember to ... *exhale.* You Light up this world with your great capacity to do so when you are at ease and at peace with yourself.

You have all been to the great halls where wisdom and justice merge together as one. You have all participated in the conferences We had many, many times over, as We discussed the roles each of you would play during this lifetime. The high council meetings were always abuzz as each of you chimed in with your insights on where, when and to what degree, each of Us could work together to find a common ground for you all to come together as the Gods and Goddesses you each are. Time and time again we cautioned you not to try to take on too much, but instead remain steady and true in your causes. Those of you who have chosen to keep your lives simple have in many regards had the more difficult roles to play. You each found at one time or another, sometimes for long stints at a time, that you were all alone in your thoughts and seldom had the people around you that you wanted to have with you. Many of you Walk-Ins in particular were not able to sustain the relationships that your predecessors started out with. This disrupted the families and friends of the one you had replaced. But walk alone most of you did, whether you are a Walk-In or not. There were many of you who met others who were like you, yet you still found you had to eventually separate from them. Although they may have known some of the greater truths, they were still not on your level. Many simply did not have your drive and stamina and fell to the wayside as you continued on with your missions.

Starseeds from all walks of life have felt the overwhelming sensations of being all alone too. Many of you were so wrapped up in the practical world that you truly had no idea why you always felt different and segregated from your peers or familial members. You were never meant to really fit in; your missions were to make a difference in the lives of Earth Seeds by uniquely **standing** and being unafraid to speak your truths. There has never been any grouping that incarnated in this world that has not been tested mightily about their beliefs. I marvel at all of your accomplishments both on a practical level as well as a Spiritual level. But please stop playing the "what if" game. If it helps you to make better sense of what I am telling you then examine the connotations of "IF." IF is a *possibility*, "IS," is in the realm of *probabilities* which MAY at some point become written in stone. Work with what "is," all right?

I must tell you before I leave this writing that I honor you when you fall and yet you are able to reclaim yourself and continue to move forward, just as I honor you when periods of radiance sweep over you and you find that you can see more clearly now. Never ever have any doubt about this. Just continue to BE because you have earned the right to BE. LIVE because you have earned the right to and most importantly, because you can. No matter how long or short your stay here is, I am continuing to encourage each of you to make the most of every moment by continuing to live *in* the moment regardless of what others may say about that. Remember, those who live *for* the moment, are not really living at all. Do you understand?

In loving service to you all, I dedicate this catalyst to the wonders you are Creating and the ones yet to be Created by and through YOU. *God*

God's final message - I speak with you from the Threshold of the Final Frontier, the frontier of Truth and freedom for all

God ... OK, Planetizens, well, since you have made it this far into the book, I can tell you all that you are surpassing your own expectations of yourselves! Not surprisingly however, few of you realize this. I am very grateful that you have each exercised your prerogative to continue on to the conclusion of this book. Most of you are unconscious of the fact that you are continuing on by using the fertility of your *Soul's rites of passage* to do so. You are now much better prepared to cope with and handle the strange machinations you are seeing taking place worldwide. This book was intended to do all that it could to expand and enhance all states and stages of your consciousnesses, while still bringing you to the final threshold of truth and the <u>understanding</u> of truth. It is your truth, your honor and your integrity which have kept you in balance throughout all the turmoil and emotional, physical and Spiritual violations that were endured by you each. There is nary a single Planetizen on this world that has not been hard-pressed to continue to escape those demon attacks, those sometimes deadly coercions projected at each of you by the dark children and their cohorts. It is because you are the nemesis of all that they are that you have each suffered so grievously here. Please, I do not want any of you to think for a nanosecond that just because Celestial and David are My chosen scribes for these books, that life has been easy for them because of that role here. In ways most of you will never hear about while you are still mortal, these two stalwart Souls walking in human form have suffered much more than the majority of you have!

189

I decided to inform you all of this without consulting My Celest-Self or My David-Self, because I knew that it would cause them to squirm a bit. *But,* in My role as the Luminescent of this Universe, I must say and do what I feel I must in order to be sure there are no misunderstandings about this matter. I am also doing so because I have from time to time detected some faint "mind mumblings" by a few Planetizens as well as several Earth Seeds who are evolving. These personalities seem to think that just because I select some Souls to perform this type of work for Me, that I somehow or another make their lives easier. To that I can only say, *"I wish!"* Because you each work under the auspices of Universal Laws and the Advocacy Agreement is embedded in those Laws, none of you are treated any differently than another! So it is that here where I have placed MySelf on this threshold where Truth and Honor MUST reign supreme, that I felt it necessary to clear up any misunderstanding about them and your own future projects.

In a previous book, I suggested that you each begin writing the new book of revelations; do any of you remember this? Yes, I used the term "revelations" not "revelation," because in truth the new book of revelations will REVEAL much more than the singular old style title did. Yes, I watched the head scratching and the, "oh, how am I supposed to do that?" from so many of you. Actually after you have finished reading the rest of this book, there is none among you who should not be able to finally understand that you write "revelations" through THOUGHT. Your projects are many. Now that you know the ultimate importance of your roles as Advocates and the indisputable fact that you ARE the Jesus THE Christ Consciousness along with My Jesus and Our beloved Mary Magdalene, this should aid you greatly in Creating the thought forms necessary for the final birthing of the book. You see Children; many of you are already evolving to a singular type of attunement of a particular stage of eternal

190

life while you are still mortal. This is of course what is desired by Us for each of you. But what We desire does not always happen, anymore than what YOU desired in the past has happened for you. This attunement I speak of is very important for you and to you individually and collectively. Although I will not go into a detailed description of this now, suffice it to say that this massive force is cleaning up your mental "hard drive." This force is replacing what needs to be replaced with pristine energy forms and massive electrical waves which will now continue to enhance your lives while raising your vibrations. These electrical waves are dampened down a bit so that they enter with a cohesive movement and can not in any way be harmful. These waves also respond benevolently to THOUGHT. They are steady and have a strong natural ability to integrate with body, mind and Soul. Of course they also aid in the processing of your new Light cells, thereby aiding with the continuation of the formation of your new Light bodies. That is all you need to know about that, *for now that is.*

Do not be surprised please if in but a short span of spatialness I contact some of you and ask you to write some words for Me and from Me. The Souls whose duties will include writing down all the thought forms that are being reenergized will receive instructions about how to do so and they will be informed about <u>when</u> the intersection appears for those to be placed in book form. I will personally take charge to ensure it will happen! Meanwhile, as part of your shared collective mission, write down the thoughts you have and *when the designated interval arrives,* you will discover other people that you know or will know, will share the same thoughts. NO, it is not necessary for you to know when this will happen. You do your part and I will do mine. Please try to simply remain centered in order that you can be focused on all that you now need to do. This book, Advocates for Justice, is also propelling you more rapidly into the matrix of the realm of NOW. So do not be concerned if at times your "forgetfulness" reaches a new irritating level and your inability to remember what day it really is, seems to happen much more frequently. If you know others who are experiencing this simply smile as they tell you about it and you could say, *"Welcome to the future NOW, Now."* Perhaps they will understand, perhaps they will not. What is important is that YOU understand!

OK, a great benefit you will derive from reading Advocates, although in My humble opinion the book itself is a benefit birthed in totality, there is a personal benefit that I do not want you to lose sight of. That benefit is: now that you arriving at the finale of the book, you will discover if you have not already, that this book will cause you to challenge everything you used to think and you will begin to look at everything with a new and fresh perspective. I suppose this gives a whole new meaning to, "out with the old and in with the new." I do ask each of you to always maintain your integrity and your honor and to honor truth, but do not try to defend truth or your integrity. I have said it before but it bears repeating to you now, "if you try to defend your truth or your integrity, you invalidate them." You may mull this over for a moment and see if you understand. Planetizens, regardless of where your own home worlds are, while you are still on the Earth Star planet, you must **always** and in **all-ways,** bear in mind that the dark can not exist without other varying shades of darkness. And Light-filled minds and hearts crave the Light which exists in other human Beings here. Minds that are filled with self-created illusions, or with illusions of true reality that are cast upon their minds, are the playgrounds of the dark. So it is that here on this threshold where I stand, I send you one and all limitless illuminating thoughts, and I send you streamers bathed in their own incandescent glory. I send these to you as part of your Earthly rewards and in honor of the greatness you have. Stop thinking you are merely ordinary; instead look more closely at yourselves and arrive at the realization that you are extraordinary people living extraordinary lives. When that innate understanding comes to you I ask that you cherish it, love it without imposing any conditions on it and magnify it in your own way through your freedom of expression. It is in that freedom of expression where the truest of freedom lives.

Come join Me Children, **STAND** with Me; join Me in relishing the greatest lifetime you have ever had. Simply close your eyes and imagine a place in the starry skies, in this place you will see a massive Light ball circling itself and appearing to become larger the more often you look. THAT Children, is ME. You can send yourselves to Me this way and We shall dance the dance of eternal life and experience the greatest of all majestic moments ever had. We shall proudly **STAND** and experience and share our love for one another.

As always I wish you each safe passage. May you satiate yourself with the undulating nectar of life eternal. And may your wishes become reality with no conditions imposed. The turbulent times which lie before you are much shorter than those you have previously endured. This world of Mine, My beloved Terra, will soon become the playground for the Illuminated Peaceful Warriors you each are. There will be a better life more suited for you to be able to BE the righteousness of yourselves and to shine as the beautiful Souls you each are. The yellow brick road is rapidly dissipating in the wasteland of linear time. Manifest to your heart's desire and you will surely succeed at all you set your hearts and minds to. *Just be realistic, OK?* I will be there with you, for with *Our Truth* We will traverse the stellar byways in search of Our next adventure. And life is an adventure, one to be cherished and always and in all-ways to be held in the highest regard. I look forward to hearing from each and every one of you in every NOW moment. Every thought you have of peace, of jubilation, of inspiring yourselves to BE part of the New Earth, of Creating great communities based on thought, these are but some of the times you are speaking to Me.

I salute you one and all, you who are *My Advocates for Justice*. I dedicate this book to each of you; it is but part of your birthright. *God*

God and Maria

This is a special communication
between God and Maria Nieuwenhuysen

Maria ... Dear God, if it pleases you, let me write a chapter for the "Advocates for Justice" book. I love your books. Connecting with you to write a chapter would be an honor, an upliftment and source of pride for me. Yes, God, I am happy to be included in the Advocacy. At last I seem to be doing something right.

God ... Yes, you are doing something right, but you never noticed. You always walked with your head down as if you were forced to be walking against a fierce storm and you were. You just went on doggedly. That time is over. I want you all to walk upright now. To enjoy life and being alive even if your friends are both jealous of you and laughing at you at the same time. Those who ridicule you will find themselves walking into a wall that will not budge. Many people who are well educated in universities do not want to find out that there is another reality that they don't know about and that escapes their mind that wants proof and measurements in the 3D way. You could never give that to them, even though you tried and when you almost succeeded in doing so, something blocked your efforts. And so you stood alone.

Those days are almost over. The night is almost over and the sun is close to the horizon. The skies are already lighting up. We are aware of what is happening around you. The Earth is sending her messages. The winds are talking to you.

Enjoy the new spring. The Light that is in you will support and guide you. Feel the light, feel My presence.

195

Don't let others leach out your quiet happiness. Stand straight and know that your time has come. At last.

The winds of change will blow away the old structures and limitations. You are finally being accepted for who you are. Wonders will happen around you. New animal species will make their presence known. New fruits and plants will be growing in your garden. You will enjoy the company of your fellow human beings; they will intuitively recognize the light that you carry. You will be receiving many ideas on how to create a society that is supportive for all its members. Supportive for spiritual growth and contentment, that is.

People will again know who I am and who they themselves are. You will be able to incorporate more and more of your divine heritage. People will be able to recognize truth when they hear it. You will no longer be scared for your children of what might happen if they speak of what they know and are aware of. They will amaze you with the knowledge they bring with them.

What will you do? How will you live? How will you organize your communities? Many of you have images in your minds, images of peace, beauty, oneness with nature. Once you feel the constraints of the society weaken, you will be able to make them into a reality. You will hear about the new Mozarts and the new Rembrandts. Their works of art will not be sold to the highest bidder; you will all try to devise a system that will allow everyone to enjoy them.

You will live in your communities as if you are all one family, taking care of each other as family members do. Living will be easier as your new bodies are more resistant to disease and your surroundings are once more clean and nourishing. At this moment many of you are living in bodies that suffered much from disease, a hard life, aging and the pollution that is all around you. Imagine how you would feel if you would wake up in the morning without aches and pains, full of energy and content with yourself and with your life. What would you do? Imagine if you just could shed all those feelings of tiredness, loneliness and the feeling of always swimming against the stream. Imagine not having to block hearing the fights your neighbors have, imagine not feeling you have to pick up empty beer bottles in the park or other pieces of trash. Imagine not having to watch out for your physical safety. No more viruses that attack your computer, no more phishing emails. Just honesty, valued for the space and freedom it creates.

Look at all the aspects of your life. What could all be changed to live better and feel more free? You could certainly make sure that all professions were equally valued and all the people could have an opportunity to learn or practice the work they want to do. Life does not have to be so hard. Working 40 hours a week would be way too much. Imagine a communal meeting where the work is divided and for instance the group of builders are seeing to it that everybody has a pleasant, warm and comfortable home, the gardeners are growing all the food that is needed (of course without pesticides) and another group takes care of comfortable clothing for everyone. And all are equally valued.

Such communities have existed in the past, but because the human consciousness was still at a level that was too low, they all finally failed. This time they will work. We will see to it.

Imagine science turning a new leaf. Imagine people working on problems that the community asked them to solve and sharing their inventions freely. Better cleaning systems could be invented, softer and more durable material for clothing, better ways to keep houses warm in winter, better ways to dispose of waste materials. Imagine a communal meeting where inventors show their work and citizens are asked if they want to try it and after a few weeks or months the community is shown the results of the trials. No manipulation of results, no persuasion to choose a certain way, just simple openness. Just wanting to do the best for "the family." People would be able to trust each other again. Wouldn't that be great?

Imagine living like this on planet Earth, one of the most beautiful planets of the galaxy. You will have so many resources that will help to create a new and better way to live.

What we have to do now, is to get from here to there. It looks huge and it is, but you are not aware of the plans We have laid out, you are not aware of all the help that is coming your way. I do not mean space ships landing here and doing the work for you. I mean many very evolved beings descending here to help. Some incarnate here, some walk-in and some just create a suitable body for themselves. They will keep on coming and do what it takes to Create the change.

In the past everyone who wanted to create a more loving society had to push against the prevailing disinterest or outright opposition. The situation is reversed now. The scales are swinging the other way. Proceeding with manipulation and power plays is getting harder and harder. The collective consciousness is changing. People have had enough; they are irritated by new talks of war, by the huge powers of some companies, by the greed and manipulation of the bankers. People are claiming their own power back.

There will still be a lot of victims. Some countries are beyond rescuing. Many people are too frozen in their way of life to change. They feel the changes as threatening and long for the "good old days," when life was predictable and politicians and churches told people what to do and how to view the world. People feel they are on their own now and it makes them uneasy and angry. The new world beckons them, but they prefer to look the other way. They prefer the structures of the past. That way of life will no more be available on this planet.

So My message to you is to hold on to all your lofty ideals and know that you are supported and that We will help you to make them happen. In the meantime navigate the waters of change. Each and every one of you is protected and will get all the help you need to achieve what you have set out to do in your Soul contract, unless you ask to change that contract.

When you look around the world is in a deplorable state. I will not deny that, but look at yourself. Look how much you have changed already, how much stronger you are, how your vision has cleared. You are realizing your own power, you may be saddened by the indifference and lack of understanding from the people around you, but you will no longer be victimized. You know there is a way out and you no longer have to beg and plead to deaf ears. You know change is coming, whether you can convince people or not.

So if you feel cornered, tired or stuck, picture Me standing beside you lending you My strength. Ask for help from all the sources available to you. You are our precious ground workers, you may feel you are standing alone on the battlefield, but you are supported by many unseen groups.

So shine your Light, hold on to your vision. Embellish it, enlarge it and observe it become a reality.

We are the champions in this peaceful battle. *God*

The Legitimacy of Spirit and its influence on Life

Throughout our own personal walk here on the Earth Star planet, we have observed with great irony the very strange ways so many people have of honoring professions as well as honoring the people within the professions. Scientists honor science, yet fiercely compete for awards; although only the most truthful and courageous of them will actually admit that science at best is an educated guess of unsupported suppositions, based on mathematical equations and totally unrealistic theories in most cases. What is astonishing to us though is the fact that because they are so concerned about their prestige in the scientific world, they lose sight of truth that is right in front of them. If it is not found in their scientific journals, then how can it be true? That is their perception of the legitimacy of science in life. In the medical world people are constrained to only teach what they themselves have been taught through medical books. Very few men and women are able to break through that barrier and actually consider or dare to speak out about the fact that medicine is NOT always correct. If they do they know they will be ostracized within the medical communities.

The same is true of religions. People are raised to blindly believe what their Care Takers say is true, seemingly without any consideration of the true nature of religions. Nor do they do anything about the fact that religions do not treat males and females the same way. People who are the governing bodies of religions don't want to understand that one gender is no better than another. To foolishly believe that God, by whatever name they call Him, would only choose to speak with male clerics in defining what is true and what is not, is a _true_ bastardization of the truth and has NO legitimacy. In essence they are rather blatantly proclaiming that God chooses men over women. How sad! To try to tell the religious people that this is not so, that

God treats each gender the same, would simply cause the people to recoil in horror. Why would they do that? They would do so simply because it is not what they were conditioned to believe. Do not even dare to bring up the subject of androgyny!

We could go on and on and name all other professions, but it would probably be pointless to do so. But what really rankles us the most is when we are listening to people who so arrogantly declare that only certain countries with certain nationalities are the only ones who have the ear of God. That belief is an exercise in what we call, "the illegitimate nature of Spirituality." We have spent years speaking publically and as usual very openly, defining the concept of Spirituality and sometimes, but not too often, some people actually "get it."

It doesn't matter what anyone's profession is, or what anyone is doing to help others to better understand life if the Spirituality is not present. If it is not present then it is not Spirit that is influencing life. Stop and think for a moment of what your own life would be like if you did not have the influence on your life that only Spirit can bring to you. Then think for just a moment about all the people you know who are so far removed from being Spiritual people or understanding Spiritual people that trying to compare them to true Spiritual people would be like trying to compare onions to oranges. Regardless of what you have each endured in the past years or what any of you are contending with now, if you did not have the legitimacy of your Spiritual knowledge to see you through everything, what **would** you have in life that could possibly be of greater importance? Too many people here on this planet are still being continually shocked when they see, hear or read about the shenanigans that many governments are engaged in, as well as how easily younger adults and young children are being pulled into a cesspool of illusionary reality. We would like you readers to know that each time you allow that shock to throw you off-balance you are taking a tiny step backwards. We say this because it may only knock you off-center for just one moment, but one moment is still too long. All of you who are empaths have a double type of whammy to contend with. The empathic ability is wondrous but it must be kept under control, otherwise it may affect you in ways you do not yet understand. We ourselves as empaths know only too well that we must protect ourselves from the myriad emotions emanating from people around the world. If we do not, it drains our energy banks and it could cause physical damage, so we too must be careful!

Think of the term, "legitimacy." The absolute nature of legitimacy is that it does conform to recognized rules or traditions. However, when it is the legitimacy of Spirit, it is an energy conforming in a nonconformist way to a Higher Power. The legitimacy of Spirit reigns supreme because it is part of a higher knowing, a truer understanding of the nature of all that is Divine. It is in this particular manner that the all pervasive, all persuasive force of Spirit not only influences life, but can and does also function as a fulcrum which stabilizes the very foundation of life.

We will be so happy when all people here can not only understand this, but will realize that living a Spiritual life is the only way to truly have a life.

We applaud all Advocates for Justice; all that we do here both individually and collectively will usher in the most wondrous of times. You _have_ the legitimacy of Spirit; now please go on to influence life.

Salude ... Celest and David

Biographies

Celestial Blue Star and David of Arcturus ... We have been working with God since the Creation of our Souls. Upon our final return to Source we want to be able to look at ourselves and know that we left no stone unturned in fulfilling our designated missions. Our missions have been and always will be to be in service to God and to the other Luminescents. We feel honored to be here now at such a pivotal point in Earth's history. We are in service to you and all of humanity just as we have always been. Welcome to the Jesus The Christ Consciousness, may you always and forever be one with The Christ Consciousness in the Golden NOW.

God ... I have known each person who has been reading this book since the Creation of your own Souls and I can feel the pureness of the rhythm of your heartbeat symbolizing your love for Me and your devotion to duty. May you all walk in fields of splendor with the true knowledge that I walk with you always and forever.

Books currently available from Celest and David

All books are available in paperback, PDF and e-Book

The God Book Series

1 - *And Then God Said... Then I Said... Then He Said...*Volume One

2 - *Beyond the Veil ~ Epiphanies from God*

Gods Truths and Revelations for Today and Tomorrow

3 - *And Then God Said... Then I Said... Then He Said...*Volume Two

4 - *The Code*

5 - *Beyond the Journey - Life in the Hereafters*

6 - *Advocates for Justice*

~~~~~

Blue Star the Pleiadian

"My Teachings through Transmissions"

A Three Volume Series

~~~~~

Star Tek - **Perspectives through Technology** Volume 1

Star Tek Volume 2 will be available in the near future

~~~~~

Celest and David's Websites

www.bluestarspeaks.com

www.awakenedhearts.com

www.godumentary.com

www.walk-insummit.com

New Book News

May 2013 - It was suggested that Celest and David needed to write their own books chronicling aspects of their journeys. They will do so when the God Book Series is completed.

Celest's book will be entitled *"The World according to My Celestial Self."* David's title is like life, a work in progress.

July-11-2010 was when Celest was told that God wanted us to write a complete series of His books. David later talked to God about this matter and was told that this was predestined long, long, ago. God has said that there will be a total of eight books in the God Book series.

The entire God Book series consists of:

#1 And Then God Said... Then I Said... Then He Said...
    Volume One

#2 Beyond the Veil~Epiphanies from God

#3 And Then God Said... Then I Said... Then He Said...
    Volume Two

#4 The Code

#5 Beyond the Journey - Life in the Hereafters

#6 Advocates for Justice

#7 Winter People who Ride the Wind

#8 Avatars in the Valley of the Ancients

If you wish to be added to our "private" *new book notification list* send us an email to earthstar@awakenedhearts.com

For information on how to order our books please go to:

http://rainbowproducts.awakenedhearts.com/

Note:

The God Books are currently in the process of being translated into Dutch. Check "Rainbow Products" or Update Notices on our websites for updated information about when these will become available.

CPSIA information can be obtained
at www.ICGtesting.com
Printed in the USA
BVOW03s1959211217
503398BV00001B/278/P